SHINE LIKE A DIAMOND

Compelling Stories of Life's Victories

Compiled by: Anita Sechesky

LWL PUBLISHING HOUSE
Brampton, Canada

SHINE LIKE A DIAMOND – Compelling Stories of Life's Victories
Copyright © 2017 by LWL PUBLISHING HOUSE
A division of Anita Sechesky – Living Without Limitations Inc.

All rights reserved. No part of this publication may be reproduced, distributed or transmitted in any form or by any means, including photocopying, recording, or other electronic or mechanical methods, without prior written permission of the publisher, except in the case of brief quotations embodied in critical reviews and certain other noncommercial uses permitted by copyright law. For permission requests, write to the publisher, addressed "Attention: Permissions Coordinator," at the address below.

Anita Sechesky – Living Without Limitations Inc.
lwlclienthelp@gmail.com
www.lwlpublishinghouse.com

Publisher's Note: This book is a collection of personal experiences written at the discretion of each co-author. LWL PUBLISHING HOUSE uses American English spelling as its standard. Each co-author's word usage and sentence structure have remained unaltered as much as possible to retain the authenticity of each chapter.

Book Layout © 2017 LWL PUBLISHING HOUSE

SHINE LIKE A DIAMOND – Compelling Stories of Life's Victories
Anita Sechesky – Living Without Limitations Inc.
ISBN 978-1-988867-00-7
ASIN 1-988867-00-7

Book Cover: LWL PUBLISHING HOUSE
Inside Layout: LWL PUBLISHING HOUSE

CONTENTS

LEGAL DISCLAIMER 1

FOREWORD 3

GRATITUDE & BLESSINGS 7

DEDICATION 13

INTRODUCTION 15

CHAPTER ONE 21
    Discovering Your Life without Limitations – Anita Sechesky

CHAPTER TWO 29
    Stay True to You – Elizabeth Pennington

DIAMOND LETTERS 37
    Candace Hawkshaw

CHAPTER THREE 41
    Childhood Taunts – Jasmine Jackman

DIAMOND LETTERS 51
    Leah Lucas

CHAPTER FOUR 55
    Rough Cuts – Stephanie Roy

CHAPTER FIVE 61
    A Woman's Spirit Is Her Strength – Anita Sechesky

CHAPTER SIX 71
    There is More to Life – Diana Alli D'Souza

DIAMOND LETTERS 79
    Winnie Smith

CHAPTER SEVEN 83
Restoration through God's Grace – Larissa Reed

DIAMOND LETTERS 91
Elizabeth Pennington

CHAPTER EIGHT 95
Finding the Harmony within…Once Again – Michelle LeRoy

DIAMOND LETTERS 103
Kesha Christie

CHAPTER NINE 107
What We Put out There Comes Back – Susan Kern

CHAPTER TEN 113
Hope Is a Personal Journey Within – Anita Sechesky

CHAPTER ELEVEN 121
How to Be a Friend in the Worst of Times – Elaine Cray

DIAMOND LETTERS 129
Kesha Christie

CHAPTER TWELVE 131
That Negative Energy is Unhealthy – Leah Lucas

DIAMOND LETTERS 139
Melisa Archer

CHAPTER THIRTEEN 143
Multi-Faceted Woman - How to Manage Life – Michelle Francis-Smith

DIAMOND LETTERS 151
Mary Hilty

CHAPTER FOURTEEN 153
Hiding in the Shadow of His Wings – Winnie Smith

CHAPTER FIFTEEN 159
Shining Like the Diamond I Am – Anita Sechesky

CHAPTER SIXTEEN 165
Can't Forget How Far I've Come – Mary Hilty

DIAMOND LETTERS 173
Anita Sechesky

CHAPTER SEVENTEEN 177
Diamonds on Ice – Melisa Archer

CHAPTER EIGHTEEN 183
The Hug of Hope – Sandi Chomyn

DIAMOND LETTERS 189
Susan Lawrence

CHAPTER NINETEEN 191
Pregnant At Forty-Nine – Yvonne Reid

CONCLUSION 197
Anita Sechesky

Shine Like a Diamond-Compelling Stories of Life's Victories

Compiled by Anita Sechesky

LEGAL DISCLAIMER

The information and content contained within this book *Shine Like a Diamond-Compelling Stories of Life's Victories* does not substitute any form of professional counsel such as a Psychologist, Physician, Life Coach, or Counselor. The contents and information provided does not constitute professional or legal advice in any way, shape, or form.

All chapters are written at the *discretion* of and with the full accountability of each writer. Anita Sechesky – Living Without Limitations Inc. or LWL PUBLISHING HOUSE is not liable or responsible for any of the specific details, descriptions of people, places or things, personal interpretations, stories and experiences contained within. The Publisher is not liable for any misrepresentations, false or unknown statements, actions, or judgments made by any of the contributors or their chapter contents in this book. Each contributor is responsible for their own submissions and have shared their stories in good faith to encourage others.

Any decisions you make and the outcomes thereof are entirely your own doing. Under no circumstances can you hold the Compiler, LWL PUBLISHING HOUSE, or "Anita Sechesky – Living Without Limitations Inc." liable for any actions that you take.

You agree not to hold the Compiler, LWL PUBLISHING HOUSE, or "Anita Sechesky – Living Without Limitations Inc." liable for any loss or expense incurred by you, as a result of materials, advice, coaching or mentoring offered within.

The information offered in this book is intended to be general information with respect to general life issues. Information is offered in good faith; however, you are under no obligation to use this information.

Nothing contained in this book shall be considered legal, financial, or actuarial advice.

The author or Publisher assume no liability or responsibility to actual events or stories being portrayed.

It may introduce what a Life Coach, Counselor or Therapist may discuss with you at any given time during scheduled sessions. The advice contained herein is not meant to replace the Professional roles of a physician or any of these professions.

Shine Like a Diamond-Compelling Stories of Life's Victories

Compiled by Anita Sechesky

FOREWORD

I am deeply honored to write the foreword for Anita Sechesky's newest treasure, and soon-to-be best-selling book Shine Like a Diamond – Compelling Stories of Life's Victories. A compilation of not only her own personal inspiring and courageous stories, but her continued wisdom to share captivating anthologies, this particular book with nineteen other co-author gems across the Globe. You won't want to put this tear-jerking, awe-inspiring book down, as has been my experience. You will feel your own personal pain through harrowing times, yet you will soon find out that you too are going through the process of being transformed into a precious diamond, bursting forth to shine all of what makes you priceless to the world. Altogether, these twenty empowered women stand with you marching in solidarity. You will find solace through their strength, resilience, and determination to heal from all kinds of life crises and challenges. They are my "sheroes", my pearls of wisdom; courageous and powerful changemakers. They too were burdened with many challenges and threats. I use past tense, but let me emphasize that some continue to march onwards despite the junk dumped on them. "You wanna shine like a diamond; you gotta get cut like a diamond!" (Eric Thomas)

Like the most precious gem, unearthing *Shine Like a Diamond – Compelling Stories of Life's Victories* dovetails brilliance and radiance in every chapter. You will thread through many lessons of empowerment, resilience, and grit. I myself have faced many hardships in my life, too tragic to even think about, yet, like our authors, I wake up each morning thanking my Higher Being for gifting me with the remarkable ability to tolerate distress, and accept each day filled with GRATITUDE that I am alive to be surrounded by my children, nine beautiful grandkids, family, friends, and those who just need a pillar to lean on. I made it; now it's my time to help awaken the great spirit hidden in them. Hard times storm our way when we least expect them, yet with determination and new found confidence we are ready to stand up and fight the right revolution, we can weather the storms, and I believe we can be comforted in your faith and mine.

Don't let anyone steal your joy away from you. Shine, Shine, Shine Like a Diamond. I empathize with many unique individuals, particularly women whose lives have been devastated with hopelessness, no breathing room to release the chains of bondage. Thanks to the great advocates and organizations embarked on social justice and responsibility such as the Global Women's Project with a powerful mission of opening doors for women: "We believe in the power of women to change their lives, their communities and the world. Yet too many women are prevented from enjoying their full human rights because of poverty, discrimination, violence and inequality. We want to see a world where every woman can determine her own life. We work alongside local women-led organizations to provide women with opportunities to learn, earn an income, and lead the change they want to see. Join us because #womencantwait." So many women and their families live through tough conditions, far harsher than we can imagine. I am very confident that the stories you read in this book will resonate deeply within you and achieve the goal of empowering so many others. You will feel compelled to gift this book to a friend who will find a story that will also awaken their soul to Shine, Shine, Shine Like a Diamond.

Diamonds are a great example of beauty and strength. Women rarely pat themselves on the back for all they have endured in life. Ladies, you are invaluable and priceless, rich in all you bear on your shoulders. We are precious, resilient human beings, begging to be refined. "A diamond's creation requires immense pressure and intense temperatures to reach its highest potential. Without enduring the adversity and pressure of its environment, the diamond would never become the treasure it was meant to be. May the changes you grow through bring incredible value in helping you forge a remarkable and multi-faceted life." (Susan C. Young).

I have worked on my diamond, enchanted with its sparkle and shine. It took me more than six decades to realize that I had the right to glisten. Yes, I am a phenomenal diamond, gleaming more than the one on my pinky finger, glistening with pride. I pay homage to all those who caused the friction, and to the many women and men who broke a window, got me out of the rut, and opened a door filled with hope and opportunities to restart and reignite my claim to fame. Yes, I twinkle and glitter reassured that resilience, self-reliance, and desire for self-determination to reach for the stars are cosily sitting in the palm of my hand next to the flashing tiny diamond! Happily retired, I now run my own Foundation that makes a difference around the Globe, and enjoy my new-found passion to teach the most vulnerable indigenous children of all age groups in the Himalayas, India. You see, I have now chosen to learn the art of a diamond cutter helping many dazzle out of miserable situations.

I am blessed to have found Anita Sechesky, a sister from another mother, a mentor I look up to. She is that perfect Diamond who shined into my space and time. I believe in Divine Intervention. I met Anita, personally, on a Toronto talk show, where she was being interviewed along with myself. I was focusing on Philanthropy and Humanitarianism around the Globe, and she was proud to highlight several of her best-selling books, Absolutely YOU! – Overcome False Limitations & Reach Your Full Potential being one of them. Our souls connected, and our minds have found ways to inspire the world with the work we do. She is certainly one of the best global publishers representing her company, LWL PUBLISHING HOUSE. Anita is a highly-skilled Registered Nurse, a Certified Professional Coach, Key-note Speaker, workshop trainer & MasterClass facilitator, Conference Host and Founder of Living Without Limitations Conferences, a dynamic Visionary & Book Writing Mentor. Anita is a positive force to reckon with. She is a self-motivated leader who has been the guiding force in collectively bringing hundreds of Visionaries from across the Globe, over the last five years, to tell their stories. She believes that we are filled with so much potential. To me she is the female version of Wayne Dwyer, bless his soul. In this case, your Diamond life is ready to shine as you go from one chapter to the next.

Blessings dear readers! "Diamonds are proof that the most valuable things are sometimes formed in the dark." (Matshona Dhliwayo). Don't be afraid to sparkle even brighter. When you are feeling the pressure of life, remember that you are just getting your shine on.

Be resilient, tough, powerful. No matter what, you too are strong enough to go through the process of being shaped into a unique DIAMOND. Take a bow! You earned it! Namaste!

Diana Alli D'Souza, O.Ont,

President, Access Empowerment Council (www.accessempowermentcouncil.org)

Winner of multiple distinguished awards including the most prestigious Order of Ontario and Queen's Diamond Jubilee Medal

Compiled by Anita Sechesky

GRATITUDE & BLESSINGS

It is with sincere appreciation and gratitude that I take this time to acknowledge the people who have stood by, supported, and continually blessed and loved me for exactly who I am. Your support has not gone unnoticed and I am a better person today because of you. Through all things, I am always blessed because of the peace of God and the blanket of love that continually surrounds me and lifts me up, no matter how I may be feeing.

Thank you, Stephen, the love of my life for believing in me and my desire to always strive for greater purpose in all that I do. Your unconditional love, support, and friendship have inspired me on this journey. Thank you for helping me to establish LWL PUBLISHING HOUSE and standing by me and my vision to make this dream come true as a legacy for our children's children.

To my eldest son, Nathaniel Thomas: Thank you for being such a wise and inspiring young man. I'm very proud of you and your accomplishments. You are always a great help in so many ways as a big brother and son. I'm so grateful how I see much of myself in you, in the areas of academics and reading. My desire is that you will develop a passion for learning and helping others. As you grow you will learn that it is up to us to see the blessings in others, as many are not looking anymore. I thank God for you and how you are growing into such a bright and responsible young man. You inspire me daily. Never let anyone make you feel inferior and incompetent. Learn, listen to what others say, and don't take anything personal unless it's building you up. People love to point out what may appear as weakness in others as they elevate themselves in their own eyes. Educate yourself and apply your wisdom and skills to everything you do. Don't let anyone tell you that you cannot become the best you possible; you are always a winner! Respect and appreciate others always, regardless of their behaviors. What people do is always a reflection of what's going on inside of them. People project their issues more than they should. Everyone is accountable for their attitudes and actions regardless of who they are. It's not up to us to judge or criticize as everyone is dealing with themselves the best they can. God sees everything. You were a success from the day you were born. You are perfect to me, Daddy, and your brother Sammy, and I have always believed in you. Love Mom.

To my youngest son, Samuel Jordan: Thank you, my darling son, for the joy that you bring to all of us. You never cease to amaze me with your growing wisdom, curiosity, and skills. Sammy, you are my little songbird, so happy and free-spirited. Thank you for helping to keep me balanced with the stresses of life. You are absolutely perfect! Thank you for showing us how beautiful life really is despite anything else that may be going on around us. Your child-like perceptions bring us so much joy and happiness. Everything you do will be a success. God has great plans as you are growing into the person that you were created to be. You are perfect and success is in every step that you take. I'm so proud to call you "My little darling." Daddy, Nathaniel, and I love you and believe in you. Love Mommy.

To my beautiful, gentle, and loving mom, Jean Seergobin: Thank you so much for always encouraging me to strive for excellence in everything that I do. I love you so much with all my heart. You have shown me many things in life, especially about knowing who believes in you and that when you have that gift within you, nothing else matters. I thank you for never giving up on me, mom. It is because of you that I have learned to be strong and still have empathy and care for others. You have always stood by my side and have given me the solid strength when things were so difficult, sometimes next to impossible to keep believing in myself. Thank you for being my best and closest friend by speaking hope, love, and courage into my life, and for your heartfelt, endless prayers and never changing towards me when so many have and walked out. Thank you choosing to be my mom when you could have given up on me in the early years. Thank you, mom, for everything that you do. I love you so much.

To my dearest Dad, Jetty Seergobin: Thank you for believing in me when you didn't understand why I do the things I do. Thank you for teaching me to reach for higher goals in life and to carry on despite whatever circumstances I may be facing. Thank you for being the solid rock in our family. You've been there to help me when no one else could. Your kindness, generosity, and love cannot be put into words, Dad. I honestly don't know how I could have made it this far without having both of my parents in my life. Your love for your family is priceless and I am grateful for all that you have done as an example to help me and encourage me. Your patience in me is what has given me hope when so much hope was gone. Thank you for believing in me and my company LWL PUBLISHING HOUSE. For me, if only one life is shifted and healed through our books and given a new way to get through their heart-breaking situations with forgiveness, love, peace, and hope, then my vision to empower and bringing healing is fulfilled as it is a blessing for me to know what I could not do for our precious Jasmine Rose, is being done through these books we bring into the world. I believe somehow her memory is kept alive through these self-healing publications.

Mom and dad, I love you both so much because of your unconditional and unfailing love for me. You are my super-heroes, because both of you have encouraged, inspired, motivated, and blessed me in so many ways that have contributed to the successful person I've now become. I am ever so thankful for your unfailing love and prayers over my life and my family. It is because of your unlimited love and support towards me that I am inspired and encouraged to dream more, learn more, do more for others, and still grow emotionally stronger through my own experiences. I pray God's richest blessings of love, of good health, strength, healing, wholeness as well as joy, peace, and happiness to continue over you both for many, many more long and prosperous years. May the grace of God's divine love and the protection of his grandest angels always encamp around you and your loved ones. I love you Mom and Dad.

To my dear brother, Trevor Seergobin: Thank you for being who you are to me and my family. I pray that God's blessings overtake you and help you in every area of your life. You deserve to be blessed always. It is my greatest desire that you can see how much potential you have within yourself and that nothing is impossible as you have often told me. Always know that you are loved and greatly appreciated.

To my dear friend, Sandi Chomyn: Thank you for always believing in me when I was processing and contemplating many things. Thank you for your many prayers for me and my family. Thank you for crying with me when times were rough and allowing me to be myself in the worst way possible. Thank you for always speaking hope into my life when I wanted to walk away so many times. You were there when I was going through some very difficult times and I am so grateful that God brought you into my life when He did. You are blessings in more ways than one and the sister I never had. I appreciate you and am so grateful to have a friend like you. I believe in you too! Please know you are always in my prayers and loved more than you realize.

To my dear friend and mentor Diana Ali D'Souza: Thank you writing the Foreword for this beautiful book. There are many people that come into our lives and make so many promises, yet when it's time to see those words come to life, nothing transpires. Not with you my dear friend. Since I have had the privilege to know you, you have shown me what integrity means by the way that you live your life and stand on your promises. This is what separates the best from the rest. Thank you for being the beautiful light of inspiration that you are to not only me but so many around the world. I am honored to call you a friend. What more can I ask for than having friends who are more like family, who are compassion-filled individuals. You are a blessing.

Thank you to everyone who has been a part of my journey to get to this point. For all the people who have been part of my life, supported my dreams and ambitions, thank you for always believing in me. You see, it's never been all about me. It's about you as well and each one we are connected with.

I love and appreciate each one of you for who you are. I am truly grateful for every individual who has contributed to the woman that I am today. I apologize if I have not mentioned your names, as there may be too many to mention. You may have been that special individual who commented on one of my social media posts, maybe you sent me a personal message of encouragement when I really needed to hear it, or you told me how impressed you were with my accomplishments and encouraged me to continue despite any struggles and heartaches I may have been facing in that moment of time. Lastly, you may have been that person who purchased one of my books and it really affected you in a positive way, so much so that you felt compelled to reach out and say, "Thank you Anita for your beautiful words of hope and inspirational vision. It's really made a difference in my life." Please know you are never forgotten. All of you have impacted me greatly, and for that I am grateful. I did not have a huge cheering squad stand behind me all these years to speak encouragement into my life. In fact, I have many living family members who refuse to acknowledge me or any of my accomplishments. I have forgiven them and send love their way. I thank God for those who have come alongside of me. You have become the family I do not have. For this you must know you are always in my prayers.

I will also mention that there were many seasonal friendships that have showed up for a short time and for that I acknowledge and appreciate you for sharing that moment of your life with me. I have not forgotten you nor the experience and what it has taught me, whether good or bad. You also hold a special place within my heart.

Once again, I would like to give an unusual appreciation to those who have caused me great heartache, disappointments, and even deep emotional pain. You were the lessons that I needed at that time, so that I could become a better person today. Because of you, I will never give up in life. It was because of those hardships you caused me, that have made me strive even more to believe in hope, forgiveness, peace, and love – all of which are lacking in our beautiful and hurting world.

Two wrongs never make a right. I choose to forgive.

Love always covers a multitude of sins. 1 Peter 4:8

Compiled by Anita Sechesky

DEDICATION

The one thing about this life that is certain: many people will let you down. Does this mean that you stop living? No – never stop living because your life is not about them or for them. Your life is for those who need your love, your attention, your kind words, your special favor, your forgiveness, your gentleness, your hope, your message, your peace, your uniqueness, your leadership, your written words, your laughter, your gift, your song, your tears, your creativity, your curiosity, your presence, your enlightenment, and how you show up in the world.

Thank you, Mom, for all you have helped me to become today, tomorrow, and always. You are my precious diamond. You are my beautiful queen and my life is better because you have crafted me from your own womb to become the woman I am today.

Thank you to all mothers around the world on behalf of all your daughters you have taught, guided, prayed for, blessed, encouraged, lifted up, nourished spiritually, mentally, and physically, and given hope to when all hope was lost. You are all the priceless diamonds that we become because of who you are.

Thank you to the mothers who have angel babies, no babies, spiritual babies, and human babies. Your life experiences have raised up strong men and women with hearts and souls. What our world needs is love – it's within you to give unselfishly. You are the diamonds in the sea of Universal healing.

With Love,

Anita Sechesky

Compiled by Anita Sechesky

INTRODUCTION

When I think of an empowered woman, I think of all women around the world, the wives, mothers, grandmothers, aunts, cousins, and sisters. Not of a particular race, religion, or orientation. Nor do I imagine one body type: short, tall, slim, medium or heavyset, dark or light colored skin, straight or curly hair. For me, I look at the essence of what being a woman really is, which is the combination of her mind, body, and spirit. This is what truly makes a person who they are; not skin color, language, education, heritage, or social status.

From the time I was a young child growing up in a small isolated Northwestern Ontario community (a far cry from my luscious and tropical birthplace of Georgetown, Guyana), I have searched both inside my heart and soul, and outside in the environment I was growing up in, to find out who I really am. What am I supposed to look like? What should I wear? How do I present myself? My journey has led to hurtful places of rejection amongst people I thought would accept me because I am, after all, a "female" just like them, but unfortunately many people want to identify with their "own kind" no matter how far we may go in becoming a society based on equality for all. This has been the ongoing dilemma I have observed on social media and in the world. I see this very attitude continue in so many ways and innocently provoking the very nature of the human spirit to stand up for what they believe is right or what they feel they deserve. I have nothing against improving one's life and the quality of how you live your life, but it is rather disturbing when I see any kind of division and calling together of the individual races to stand up, show up, and speak up. I don't believe in the harshness – there is a time to be bold in one's journey and there is a time to be appreciative of what has been already historically achieved. To think differently is creating a negative mindset where there should be none.

For me, regardless of who is doing it, it brings back many memories of feeling left out and lonely in a world I was subjected to this Canadian environment based the best interests of my parents. When nothing is said about these negative and accepted events taking place, people will silently and naively continue the self-segregation by passing on the attitudes of low self-esteem, and negativity to the next generation, sadly disregarding what has already accomplished though peace and war so many years ago by lives that are not being respected for their sacrifices to make this world a better place for all.

I guess what I'm trying to say is please reconsider those events which only nominate and celebrate a certain type of people. Don't let your whole world revolve around these types of events because what will eventually happen is your perspective will become so narrow-minded, you will slowly forget that all people matter, all life comes from a woman's womb regardless of what nationality she is, what language she speaks, the color of her skin, her hair type, etc.

All human blood is the same color and regardless of the blood types, each ethnic race has every different blood type as well, so we are already equal underneath our skin. It's up to us to see this and make our attitudes reflect that of human unity and acceptance of all. The woman is a special gift to all. She is the source of life and without her, there is no life to sustain the human race. We are all one and the same. Acceptance begins within each one of us. Go ahead and celebrate your cultural differences and uniqueness – it is what makes you who you beautifully are. But please don't become so absorbed that you forget we all need each other on this planet to live in unity – after all, there is only one race – the human race!

This leads me to "Why" I compiled this long-awaited book, which is very dear to me because it covers so many facets of a woman's heart, hence the real meaning of the title "Shine Like a Diamond -Compelling Stories of Life's Victories." For me, it has been within my spirit for longer than I can remember to write about why it is so heart-wrenching to be a woman. You see, women are very hard on each other and because we often times are so fixed in our mindsets and behaviors, we are difficult to convince otherwise. What I really mean to say is that we take each other for granted and expect more than we should even though we would never consider ourselves to be accountable for the same level of expectation. We always think we can do better and if some other woman is rocking her stuff, we have a deep desire to either compete with her or be jealous because we didn't do it first. When we should be building each other up, we look for the pettiest of things to point our fingers at and suddenly that woman is the worst "bitch" there ever was. We cut off relationships like we change our undergarments and we spitefully use and speak badly of other women because we don't like something about them or maybe we don't think they deserve what they've achieved or gained in life. We take credit for something that is not ours to own, yet we would never like it if someone did the same towards us because we always think we are so much better than them. We say we forgive, but we keep talking down about our sisters until we have stomped them into the ground. We make promises we don't keep and get mad when others let us down. How could they? We assume things so easily about other women yet we have no clue what they are living through, walking through, and enduring on their journey. As women, we do and don't live like sisters. When we have faith, we are the first to doubt and steer the whole crowd wrong, yet we never humble ourselves and walk in meekness. As women of strength, we are the first to lose our words of encouragement when we see other women needing support to go through their own labour pains to victory. As women of honor, we are the first to lose our integrity by gossiping, back-biting and putting others down. I have experienced all of this in some way or another in my life whether it was in my own family or among peers and even clients. Women are mean!

So why do women deserve to be encouraged to Shine Like a Diamond and celebrated for being a woman? It's certainly not for all these negative, damaging, and destructive traits that each one of us as women possess. You might be the nicest person on the block, but I'm sure there is some other woman out there that would sadly say otherwise about you. God bless you sweetheart. I have learned in my own life journey that people will always project what they are on you. You may never hurt a single insect, but someone will say otherwise of you. People don't always want to now the truth which would set them free from their own limited mindsets, instead they prefer to be content with something they are familiar with. That is why I went to great lengths to describe so many personality traits and behaviors above. They are merely descriptive words that represent an identity that is either true or false. It is up to us individually to determine which of these representations truly reflect who we are and how we show up in the world as women filled with integrity, courage, and faith who are emotionally balanced in body, mind, and spirit.

Trust me, I've had my own emotionally weak moments in my hairdresser's chair feeling like I should start my own group and empower "my own kind." After all, it's what everyone else is doing! Then I quickly come back to reality and realize had my beautiful daughter Jasmine Rose lived to see what I was contemplating at that very moment, it would break her heart. You see, my children are both Guyanese, mixed with an east Indian heritage, and Caucasian mixed with Canadian, English, and Polish descent. With so much world travel and international business and trade over these past decades, the rise of inter-racial marriages have risen significantly and will continue as mixed children marry other mixed children creating even more beautiful "global" babies. This brings me back to my very question "Why are there so many ethnic groups promoting 'All _____ ' events and no one is saying anything?" If it was organized and promoted as an "All white" event, there would be so much chaos and confusion. Please don't allow yourself to be caught up in the Spirit of Division, because it really is a spirit that takes hold of a person's mindset, bringing in their friends called hate, jealousy, and animosity and all their other friends. Just like the saying goes, "Show me who your friends are and I will show you exactly what you are."

This book was beautifully created from the heart strings of each one of my contributors, who decided they wanted to be part of something bigger than themselves.

The stories and inspirations in this book are aligned to the vision that God placed into my heart at a very young age. I knew what it felt like to be the one who didn't fit in. I was different in my physical appearance as my family immigrated to Canada from Guyana, South America when I was just a young child at the sweet age of four. My skin tone reflected the beautiful golden hue of being born a warm, lush, and tropical country. There, I had already been introduced into Nursery School system with great friends. I was accepted and loved for who I was. I remember going out when it rained tropical buckets – there were huge mud puddles to jump in afterwards. My once playful and carefree life was instantly transformed as we relocated to Northwestern Ontario, Canada. I had to learn a whole new way of adapting into a society that was in the middle of a winter deep freeze with temperatures ranging from minus 25 to minus 40 below. Yes, it was a very brutal cultural shock for all of us. Not only was the climate cold, we soon discovered that the citizens in that part of the world were not the warmest at times either.

So you see, my vision for "Shine Like a Diamond – Compelling Stories of Life's Victories" is something that has always been a part of who I am as a person. When I grew up, I trained to become a Registered Nurse who cares for all people regardless of race, color, religion (creed), gender, age, national origin, or disability. There is no discrimination in health care just as there shouldn't be in all the other areas of our lives.

I learned tolerance at an early age. My life training involved understanding that a huge part of acceptance towards others encompassed searching my own heart to understand that people are always going to respond based on how they are feeling and what their personal experiences are. Who am I to judge? My parents are my heroes in every sense of the word. They have taught me to accept people who would never accept me and to forgive others who would never forgive me. You see, life is all about choices. Love and peace are unlimited because they come from God, whose profound peace is unlimited towards us. The more love you give, the more you get back. It may not come from where you imagine but it always does come back to find you and lift you up when you least expect.

Every one of the passages within this book come from viewpoints that are quite incredible when you really begin to understand that each person we encounter is on a journey of discovering who they are as well. We are all connected some way by our energies and ultimately in a spiritual sense. I have invited each of my contributing writers to search deeply within their hearts and souls, permitting themselves to safely bare their emotions about where they once were and compare it to where they are today. Hope, Love, and Peace along with Faith are all energies as much as they are words and emotions to put into practice and take hold of in one's life. It always surprises me how the human spirit is so strong and resilient to endure the things we face but not always brave enough to talk about without possibly feeling shame, embarrassment, or fear of ridicule.

Personally, my faith and positive mindset brought me through so many unpleasant and often times despairingly awful experiences in life, although I admit it was the love and awareness that I have very precious people who appreciate me for who I am. I never take that lightly as my own parents were both raised with only one parent figure in their lives at a young age, and they still became the best parents they could be for my brother and I, despite their lack of full parental influence. Many times, people do not realize that the reason they are struggling is due to the love and peace missing somewhere in their emotional make-up, whether it is from a parent, child, spouse, relative, or friend. Choosing to live a life filled with Hope is what connects all of our positive interactions in the bigger picture.

For those who are still lacking courage in your lives or you cannot find a way to heal the emptiness, and have become so discouraged, my message for you is never give up! You are like that Diamond in the rough – your life experiences are making you stronger and helping you to come out shining brighter. What you seek will always find you. You will come across people in this life who will only point out your weaknesses or mistakes as they see it. Don't react, instead accept it. You are beautifully created and perfect but you are evolving each and every day, so you're allowed to be imperfectly perfect. It's what gives you the human edge and it's what makes you better the next time around. Let people judge you and project themselves in your evolution. It's the best they can do and it's their weak and insecure way of trying to hold you back in life. It never works if you let it all go and keep moving in the direction of your dreams. Forgive those who have damaged your perspectives and dreams. You can still appreciate that there is a world of like-minded individuals waiting to embrace you in warmth and acceptance. Hope is what the world needs, and just like a priceless Diamond never loses in value, you are only getting better and better. Keep grinding through and allow your Creator to refine you in the beautiful light of love where you will shine even brighter!

Anita Sechesky

Chapter 1
Discovering Your Life without Limitations

When you've come to a place in your life where you feel like you're trapped or struggling, you will begin to feel constraints or chains that are preventing you from spreading your wings to fly. Many of my colleagues, friends, and clients have expressed these same kinds of feelings, not understanding why their lives seem to feel like a losing battle of unknown origins. Limitations are things that can start from early childhood and continue building up until they become walls that literally close you off from living up to who you are and stepping into your true potential.

In a sense, it may feel like you're trapped in an iron bird cage with no open doors allowing you the freedom to fly away. You can see everyone else succeeding, achieving, and satisfied in life, but with your own limiting beliefs surrounding you, life is already feeling hopeless and dangerously discouraging. You know you have greatness within you, but maybe you haven't been told so enough by those who you feel really matter. You believe there is potential for everyone, but you've adapted the mentality or belief that you're not good enough or you're just not meant to live the way you really want to.

As a Certified Professional Life Coach and a Registered Nurse with diverse knowledge and skills from various backgrounds, I've become aware of how people allow so many things to cloud their personal perceptions of their own potential in life. I love to assist my clients by guiding them to express where they feel their low points are and how these limitations have taken root like nasty weeds choking out the very life within. I ask them powerful questions and reframe situations to help them shift their perspectives. To be successful in their personal journey of evolving into their greatness, my clients are encouraged to face their boundaries headfirst, enabling them to find their courage and belief system that permits them the determination to achieve a life full of unlimited possibilities. My clients discover their own limitations by simply answering my questions or completing assessments.

When my clients express how their dreams look, feel, and even "taste," excitement sets in, but sometimes it doesn't last very long because there is a lot of personal emotional work to be done in releasing deep fears and memories that have been ingrained from life's experiences. Once they begin identifying what has caused stagnation and pain for so long, goal-setting is attainable. Life becomes liveable and not avoidable, they start to determine what their goals and ambitions look like, and this is where I help them to break it into bite-size pieces. When they taste the pleasure of achieving these small goals, the prize of success comes in closer and is visualized as realistic now. Goals are dreams that develop inside of us before we even have the skills and abilities to achieve them. My clients work through a series of various exercises building up their confidence which usually exposes the most profound limiting mindsets. As they tear away the layers of fears, unforgiveness, and pain, trapped emotional energy gets released in the form of tears or jubilation. They realize they are free to set new goals once thought as unreachable dreams. The things that were once weighing them down emotionally and spiritually are now gone.

Through "The Act of Forgiveness," I have mentored many people who have had the most profound breakthroughs. Realistically, we cannot change anyone; we can only change ourselves. Disappointments happen, but they don't need to be the focus of a life seeking joy and fulfillment. Moving forward, they realized situations once perceived as negative experiences may not have been as harsh.

You see, when living a life with a limiting mindset, everything around you becomes a misrepresentation of what your life can be. You may feel small or you're in a losing battle with life. Learning to shift your perspectives will help you to feel validated and heal so much quicker than struggling for years on your own. What you carry around inside of you emotionally is what you will attract into your life. You'll only be focused on what you feel.

Here are some key questions about limiting mindsets and perceptions in life:

Limitations Questionnaire

1) Q – Have you ever experienced poor treatment in your life by others?

    A – You may have a baggage of limitations.

2) Q – Do you feel like you're spinning in circles and not going anywhere?

    A – You have no clear direction. More than likely you have a limitation in your life preventing you from succeeding.

3) Q – Do you feel like you're like that bird in the cage?

    A – Your limitations are an invisible cage. Your wings are meant to fly.

4) Q – What kind of environment are you subjecting yourself to?

    A – This could include your exposure to destructive or harsh entertainment (movies, books, and video games), abusive or neglectful relationships, substance abuse, toxic work environments, or adverse living conditions.

5) Q – What does your self-talk look like?

    A – Allowing negative self-talk from yourself or others is destructive to self!

6) Q – How do you show up in the world?

    A – Presentation is key to success. Don't limit yourself. Take the extra time that's needed to pull your look together.

7) Q – Do have a hard time forgiving others?

    A – Holding on to resentment and anger will only cause you harm by blockages in your personal perceptions.

My clients have learned that certain lifestyle exposures will directly affect their attitudes, emotions, or health. Many people are still afraid of stepping out of their comfort zone, staying trapped by that invisible bird cage.

Life Without Limitations Questionnaire

1) Q – Are you confident enough to achieve success without permission?

    A – Living without limitations does not require consent from others.

2) Q – Do you have a dream?

    A – You have been given a gift from your Creator that's all yours.

3) Q – Can you see your dream happen?

    A – When you envision your dreams coming to life, you create your realities.

4) Q – Do you have goals hidden inside that direct your steps?

    A – Clear, concise, and achievable goals equal success.

5) Q – Do you speak positively?

    A – Positive sel-talk and reinforcement increases self-esteem and confidence.

6) Q – Do you step out of your comfort zone?

    A – You can't show up in life if you don't step out.

7) Q – How does it feel when you forgive others?

    A – Forgiving others releases personal bondages and limiting beliefs about life and people in general. Forgiveness heals!

Many people around us who have achieved success in their lives have learned at some point that they can do it. They didn't wait for permission to be the best that they can be. They didn't let their fear of failure stop them. In fact, it is common knowledge that many people who do succeed have failed many times and learned from their own mistakes, or the mistakes of others.

I allow my clients to express their concerns and help them to understand where their limitations or despair are coming from. We may set goals which are entirely client-focused and accountable to me, the coach. With this type of professional relationship, I help my clients explore their own paths in life and what speed they want to move forward.

Clients facing extreme limitations may have a great need for emotional release when trapped by their own or others' limiting beliefs. A number of them have dealt with all kinds of negative life experiences, such as the loss of a loved one, lost finances, job termination, health setbacks, divorce, physical, verbal, or mental abuse, and even racial limitations. I have observed how this affects their self-worth and confidence. When they become more focused, they learn how to heal and maintain balance in their lives to be able to be the best for their loved ones.

Food for Thought!

1) Consider adapting "The Art of Forgiveness" into your life. This is done by setting time aside to reflect on life events that resulted in unpleasant and negative unresolved feelings. This is one of the "Biggest" doors to opening limitations in life. Everything will be affected by those negative feelings: your choices, attitudes, and your health if you let it fester for too long. It may possibly show up as different forms of stress or anxiety leading to more serious health conditions.

2) You have to understand and accept that Forgiveness is needed as you cannot change the past or even other people. You can only change yourself. Decide to recall and write down the names of these people who have hurt or let you down.

3) When you have listed as many that come to your mind (it doesn't matter how far back you go), start saying, "I forgive….." "I now release all of the pain, disappointment, and heartache they have caused me."

4) Once you have done this with the entire list, you may find yourself emotionally released quickly. No one should ever have power over you to that extent unless you allow it. Words and things done in the past are in the past. Words have power and negative word cycles can be broken and replaced with

positive reinforcement. We cannot change the past but we can choose to make a better future, free of pain.

5) Now that you have done this, it is time for you to recognize how amazing and POWERFUL you really are! You are the only one who can make a difference in your life. Remove your limitations. You get to choose. Choose Love!

If anything that I have shared in this chapter resonates with you, PLEASE contact me. I believe that each one of you has "Greatness" within! Don't let labels, failures, lack, or your own limiting beliefs separate you from the joy, happiness, peace, fulfillment, and satisfaction that God and the Universe want to bless you with.

You are valued and greatly appreciated. It's time to spread your wings and fly without limitations. Living is a part of life, but it can still become a life without limiting beliefs, boundaries, and broken dreams…and that my friend is the life you really want to achieve!

Anita Sechesky is the Founder and CEO of Anita Sechesky - Living Without Limitations Inc. She is an RN, CPC, Best-Seller Publisher, Multiple International Best-Selling Author, as well as a Law of Attraction and NLPP.

Anita is also the CEO, Founder, Owner, and Publisher of her company LWL PUBLISHING HOUSE.

Currently she has successfully branded 300 International Best-Selling authors in the last three years. LWL PUBLISHING HOUSE is a division of her company, in which she offers coaching, mentoring, motivation, marketing, and of course publishing services for her clients. 2016 marks the addition of two new branches in LWL PUBLISHING HOUSE dedicated specifically to children's books of inspiration and learning, and also fiction and non-fictional single author books.

Working with Anita at one of her "LWL INSPIRED TO WRITE" workshops, Webinars or one-to-one support, will equip you to step out of your comfort zone fearlessly! Anita's solo book entitled "Absolutely You - Overcome False Limitations & Reach Your Full Potential" was written in less than four weeks and she can teach you how to do the same!

CEO of Anita Sechesky – Living Without Limitations Inc., Founder and Publisher of LWL PUBLISHING HOUSE.

Best-Seller Mentor, Book Writing Coach, Registered Nurse, Certified Professional Coach, Master NLPP and LOA Practitioner, multiple International Best-Selling Author, Workshop Facilitator & Trainer, Conference Host, Keynote Speaker.

Join my Private Facebook group: LIVING WITHOUT LIMITATIONS LIFESTYLE.

With over 960 members, we offer exclusive prizes, co-authoring opportunities, Random Contests with FREE Publishing possibilities, "Inspired to Write" Webinar classes, and more - http://bit.ly/1TIsTSm

Please visit our Facebook page: LWL PUBLISHING HOUSE

Website: www.lwlpublishinghouse.com

Email: lwlclienthelp@gmail.com.

Join my Private Facebook group:

LIVING WITHOUT LIMITATIONS LIFESTYLE: Exclusive prizes, co-authoring opportunities and Random Contests with FREE Publishing opportunities. http://bit.ly/1TIsTSm

YouTube Channel: http://bit.ly/1VEGHew

Website: www.anitasechesky.com

LinkedIn: https://ca.linkedin.com/in/asechesky

Twitter: https://twitter.com/nursie4u

Currently, we are filling co-author opportunities for all our upcoming #Hashtag

books in this series:

#Joy – *The Emotion to Embrace*

#Faith – *The Gift that Keeps on Giving*

Compiled by Anita Sechesky

Elizabeth Pennington
Chapter 2
Stay True to You

I once knew a young lady who was so eager to help everyone else with their needs that she spent most of her life doing for others and set aside things that she should have done for herself. Years later, she found herself still doing the same thing, until one day she realized time had slipped away from her.

She believed it was her "duty" to help others. After all, this is the way she was raised.

This young lady had grown up without a father – he had passed away when she was seven. She was the last born of nine children with her and two brothers the only children still in school when their father had died. All the other siblings had married and moved away, most had children of their own before she was born. She and her two brothers still at home were raised by their Mother and Grandmother.

They lived in a very small community where most everyone knew everyone else. She saw firsthand the struggles people went through just to make a living. They had to do whatever they could to earn a dollar.

She remembers one older man bringing a groundhog to their house to sell. A lady did sewing for the neighborhood for a living. Another lady did house cleaning and washing to help bring in money while her husband worked the land for their living. Men would go through the neighborhood cutting wood for the cook stoves, heating stoves, and fire places just to make a dollar. They made great sacrifices to get by from day-to-day.

Her family, as did most in the neighborhood, raised gardens and put the vegetables away for the winter months. Her family also prepared their own meat for the winter.

Everyone helped when their neighbors needed help. It didn't matter if they lived in the finest home in the neighborhood or in a "shack", a house that was ready to fall from lack of repair. It didn't have to be anything big. It could be as simple as mowing someone's lawn or something bigger like buying groceries for a neighbor when the person couldn't buy it themselves.

In her school years, she made a few friends during grade school and a few more in high school. After graduation, everyone went their separate ways, either off to college or they got married.

After graduating from high school, she went to college for only one year, got married, and then went into the working world.

She made a few friends in her working career but for the most part, her co-workers were just that – co-workers. There again with exception of a few people over the years, you called someone your friend when in fact they were only an acquaintance. So, over all, this young lady really didn't have many she would call a friend.

She joined different social activities and jumped to help every time a volunteer was needed. She participated in events to raise funds for a variety of different causes such as St. Jude's and The Cancer Society. If someone needed help with any kind of project, she was "jolly" on the spot.

She buried herself in her work. She worked extra hours with no pay just to make sure, if possible, the work would be done on time. Sometimes she did this to finish someone else's job when they left it unfinished. There were times she stopped doing her work to help others get their work finished, causing her to fall behind with her own tasks.

She tried to pay attention to everything around her to keep learning. One of her sisters had given her this advice when she had landed her first job; read everything you can, do anything you're asked to do, and help others. She followed the advice as close as she could.

Then one day she needed help. Umm…where was everyone? Well, they were too busy with "their" lives. This happened more than once. She would pamper her hurt feelings, keep them to herself, and find another way to do what it was she needed to do. You would think that if a person is kind enough to help someone when they are in need, the favor would be given in return. That's not reality – at least not for the most part. This young lady learned most people are only for themselves.

During the last few years of her career, she found herself being the highlight of gossip at work. People were saying things like "She's brown-nosing the boss." All because she gave one hundred and ten percent of her time to her work. Then it got ugly. They started harsh gossip that the young lady was doing "favors" for the boss to get promotions. They were not talking about picking up the newspaper!

The talk filtered over to activities she enjoyed and into her private life at home. People that were so called friends begin to avoid her. Some went as far as trying to use the gossip against her for their personal gain.

This caused her to become distant and on her guard always. She could hear them and sometimes see them making fun of her. She buried it deep inside and kept going. She would stand up for what she thought was right no matter the outcome which meant she found herself alone most of the time. Her world was in a tailspin all because she stood for what she thought was right.

She ignored gossip the best she could but I know she was hurt from all the negative talk. She cried sometimes for hours once she was alone. How could anyone be so cruel.

She had made friends with a lady several years earlier. They worked on committees together, attended social activities, shared traveling expenses when they needed to travel, and shared with one another about personal life events.

She stood up for the "friend" when the friend was having issues with a group of people on a committee. The "friend" was thrown out of the organization, for reasons she felt was wrong and unfair, and had no one to turn to for help. She asks the young lady if she would help her. The lady helped the "friend" and in the end the "friend" turned against the young lady. How about that?

The person, during a social event at work, walked up to the young lady and said to her, "You don't belong here." The person continued with other selfish and hateful words. Rage built in the young lady.

When the person was silent the young lady asks her if she was finished. The person said yes and the young lady asked, "Are you sure?" As soon as the person responded, "Yes," the young lady looked the person in the eyes and said, "How dare you come here and tell me I don't belong. If anyone don't belong it's you with all your lies." She continued with, "After all I have done for you, stood up for you when everyone else turned their back on you, how dare you."

Without taking her eyes off the person she told her she knew she had been spreading the gossip out of her need to fit back in with the crowd that had dumped her before. She also told her she knew who the others involved in trying to ruin her reputation and cause her to lose her job were.

It seems like the world had stopped in time. All she could see was the person in front of her. The young lady felt so much rage.

She ended with, "I know what I am, what I am not, what I do and what I don't do. My life is my life not yours or anyone else. I don't care what you or anyone says. If it makes you feel better or bigger then have at it. I know the truth and so does God."

When the young lady's adrenalin came down and she was back to herself, she looked around the room, then turned and went back to doing what she had volunteered to do. No one spoke!

This had been a first for her. She had always stayed quiet and took whatever was said deep inside and kept it private. I can say from that moment on her life began on a different journey.

She could look back and see where she could have done things differently but that's okay. That's the past.

She loved helping people; it felt natural to her. It was never a bother even when it took time away from her doing the things she would have liked to have been doing. Someone needed help and she was there. She had given her all.

Her spirit had been broken but would mend in time.

There's not enough space in this one chapter to tell her life story, that would be a book.

I've tried to write this chapter without sounding whinny or revengeful. You see the person I just wrote about is me. I am the young lady that took everything to heart like so many people do.

The purpose of my writing this chapter and sharing part of my personal life is to give encouragement to the reader. It was to be about something that I have overcome to make me the person I am today. Getting hurt from taking things to heart is one on the things I had to learn to overcome.

Facts are it hasn't taken only one thing to make me the person I am today. While the incident above caused hurt and I became skeptical of others, it made me a stronger individual. It taught me to stay true to myself. I didn't let it drag me into the other person's weakness.

The way I was raised to share and help others taught me to care for others. It taught me to be respectful of others as individuals. It put love and compassion into my heart.

I gave my all to pleasing others and in some cases, like the one above, was abused with gossip and harsh words. I spent many hours thinking it over and over in my head trying to make sense of all of it.

After all these years, I still have not found the sense of it. I know the why but not the sense of it.

People hurt each other because of jealously, greed, and all different reasons they justify to themselves. I don't get it.

Lives can be damaged beyond mending from harsh words, known as lying, and what some call "innocent" gossip – sometimes so badly, the person will take their own life.

Everything we do throughout life becomes a piece of a puzzle of our life. It's what you do with each piece that counts. Its each piece that others are influenced with, even when we aren't aware of it.

Whatever you do, whatever decisions you make, in the end, be at peace and have satisfaction that you did all you could, "little" mistakes and all.

Stay True to You.

Elizabeth is an International Best-Selling Author, PTSD and Other Trauma Coach, Certified Life Enhancement Coach, Speaker, Trainer, and Mentor. Her writing experience began with LWL PUBLISHING HOUSE. As an author, Elizabeth brings hope of confidence, strength, and love to the reader. She offers, as a coach, her clients guidance to bring balance to their life in general. Her coaching specializes in PTSD and other trauma's as well as Life Enhancement. She helps her client achieve the quality of life they desire with a technique called Neurokinesis. She has worked both in the Corporate and private sector and feels life is our best educator.

Elizabeth@cultivatenewhorizonslifecoach.com

http://www.facebook.com/elizabeth.a.pennington.3

Compiled by Anita Sechesky

Diamond Glitters of Knowledge

"A woman who is broken-hearted needs to be healed with the knowledge of how beautiful her soul really is. Allow her precious light to shine brightly by expressing everything within her heart in its own time."

~ *Anita Sechesky*

Candace Hawkshaw

Diamond Letters

Dear Diamond Sisters;

I trust this letter finds you well.

Greetings from a beautiful sunny day in Canada! I have personally been on an amazing journey and wish to share some of my wisdom with you that I have gained along the way. I was married and had three children before I was twenty-five. In that marriage and subsequent relationships, I always molded into the other person, and not myself. Because I grew up on a farm, I have always been connected to Gaia, always outside playing, singing, and dancing with her. My biggest change in life was when I reached my fifties. I call this my second life, and it truly is! I left my corporate high-end management job to live and do my passion of teaching and spreading love. Stepping out the norm and walking into the fear of the unknown was huge. I, as well as others, questioned how I would survive in a world of materialism and competition doing spiritual healing work. I knew my family and the Universe had my back, so I stepped out and did it. By leaving it, I have felt free. It has been an adventure for sure as it has helped me shed some of my old self and grown in my true self.

As you journey in this lifetime, know that you are a beautiful Divine Being and the Universe has your back. You may not see or feel it as you go through life challenges – changes, losses, heart breaks, confusion, and possibly some health issues. Many identities have been bestowed upon you since your birth – daughter, mother, sister, lover, grandmother, wife. These are all outside of you as well as all the influences that cause you to wonder who you truly are in essence. Deep within, you are Divine. Once you remember and ignite your inner spark, your life as you know it will change.

Always remember how amazing you are; how beautiful you are. Know that with daily practice you can come back to you – Thyself.

You give, give, give to all. Time to take care of you! When you start receiving and allowing yourself to say no to people or events that feel heavy inside you, you will feel a sense of freedom and feel lighter inside your whole self. Your soul will sing and dance and so many opportunities will come to you because you will be focused on you. Be your own leader. Be a teacher of others.

It is time to take back your power and to get to know Thyself. Listen to your body with all things – physical feelings, food, environments. Does your body feel light or heavy? Does it like certain foods or do the foods make your body hurt or feel sluggish?

Make a list of things in your life that you wish to do, and do them. You can do things on your own; do not wait for others. You may wait a long time.

Let your inner child out to play. Have fun. Try not to be so serious. Laugh and do things that make you fill up with joy and love.

One of the biggest shifts you can have is when you connect to nature. Get out there. Go for a walk. Listen to the sounds. Smell, feel, and pay attention to the beauty in all.

Some daily practices such as meditation assist in keeping you aligned and balanced in your mind, body, and spirit. Meditate in your own way on a daily basis, being in stillness and listening to your inner voice. After a long day at work or with people, clear your energy field. I call this energy hygiene.

When you feel as if someone is making you feel less than who you are, remember to breathe and feel in your heart your truth that you are a beautiful person.

You are made of energy like everything on this planet. It is always your choice whether or not you allow anyone's thoughts or actions about you into your energy vortex.

When you are listening to someone, actually listen and learn from them, but ensure that you stand in your integrity and speak truth always. Learn to know when to say something or not and just walk away.

Step out of fear with love. When fear enters your life, ask yourself why you are afraid. If it feels right, delete and clear that thought form. When you do something out of your comfort zone, you are actually assisting in your growth.

Everyday, either write or say gratitude for the little or big things in your life. Create a gratitude board – a vision board of what you wish in your life.

Your love for others will grow because you will have learned to love yourself. Understand we are all beautiful in our Divine essence. We are all on a journey of remembering who we are in our truth.

Hang out with those that inspire you, raise you up, support you, and those you have fun with, without any hesitation.

I wish you infinite blessings of love, joy, play, prosperity, health, love, and so much FUN! Experience life.

Take risks. Try new things. Change it up.

Explore the world out there. Go enjoy it and share your love and magic. Spread your wings and soar!

Blessings and Love

Candace Hawkshaw

Candace Hawkshaw is a certified Holy Fire II Reiki Master Teacher and a Spiritual Teacher. She is a Certified Soul Realignment Practitioner, a certified Reflexologist, a certified Acupressure Practitioner, and a certified Black Pearl Practitioner. She is an entrepreneur and her business is called Soaring Spirit. Candace has written her story in two books: *Ruby Red Shoes – Empowering Stories on Relationships, intuition & Purpose* and *Living Without Limitations – Vision Quest*. She is compiling her own anthology book titled *Love is The Most Powerful Energy in The Universe – Stories of Love's Healing Journeys* which is due to be released in August 2016.

Compiled by Anita Sechesky

Jasmine Jackman

Chapter 3

Childhood Taunts

We arrived from England with the first wave of immigrants under the new Canadian "race-free" immigration policy. My parents sought out housing in a middle-class neighborhood despite efforts by the real estate agent to redirect them to rundown areas, where there were more people like them, where they would feel more comfortable, and where housing was more affordable. But my parents wanted us to grow up in a culturally-mixed neighborhood.

Soon after we moved into our house, I remember sitting on the stoop of our home watching our neighbors move out. As an inquisitive young girl of four years old, I innocently asked the man of the house why they were moving. He stopped what he was doing, put down the box that he was carrying, looked me square in the face and said with unconcealed hate, "We don't want to live next door to a bunch of niggers!" I had never heard that word before. All I knew was that it wasn't a compliment. I just looked back blankly at my neighbor, picked up my jump rope, and ran off to play with my friends. It would be some years before the meaning of that hated word would be etched into my mind and seared into my soul.

We lived in a Maltese area in Bloor West not too far from the Junction Triangle. Scattered among the Maltese neighbors on our street were families of Polish, British, Dutch, and Russian descent, as well as a Chinese family next door to us. It was a great neighborhood. Everyone looked out for everyone's children and ensured no one got out of line. You couldn't hide. There were many eyes watching you all the time. You really felt that everyone truly cared for each other's well-being.

One neighbor of my age decided to leave us a calling card a short time after we moved in. He defecated on our front stairs right outside the main door of our porch. He wasn't too bright because he did the deed in broad daylight in the sight of other children who were all too happy to inform my parents who had left the heap of warm human feces being circled by a family of flies. Well, my mom walked right over to his house and let his parents know. His mother pulled him by his ear all the way to our house to clean up his mess. I always wondered why he did it. Was he egged on? What was he trying to say? His misstep was soon forgotten and we became the very best of friends and were inseparable so much so that our parents would joke that we were husband and wife.

Our school had no people of color and I was always the only black child in my class. I was good at sports so making friends was never a problem. I had three BFFs and we called ourselves the Four Musketeers. We serenaded our teachers hello and goodbye like a barbershop quartet; we would walk home with them and even call on them in the morning. We would plan what we would wear to school the night before and come to school wearing the same things, such as jeans and pink tops or black pants and white tops.

Then it started. Grade Five. A petulant older boy took to chasing me around the schoolyard at recess or whenever he saw me, taunting me with "nigger, nigger" and threatening to do me bodily harm. I complained incessantly to the teachers on yard duty and was repeatedly told "sticks and stones will break your bones" – so basically I was supposed to ignore him. He "niggered" and "cooned" me relentlessly for years.

By Grade Six, the novelty of being the lone black person in my grade soon lost its shine. The warranty on cuteness and innocence had worn off. I was soon to learn that I was an interloper and that there were only Three Musketeers. My one BFF, with whom I had been in every class from kindergarten to Grade Six, was having a sleepover for her eleventh birthday. I had heard other classmates speaking about the party and never once was concerned that she wouldn't invite me. We were Siamese twins attached at the hip. I instinctively felt the lack of invitation was just an oversight. Then after gym class in the presence of our other friends she said quite matter-of-factly, "I guess you've heard that I'm having a sleepover at my house for my birthday." I was fully expecting her to say, "And you're invited!" Instead she added, "My parents don't want any black people at our house, so you can't come." She turned on her heel and went off with the other girls laughing and giggling about her party. It was like a bolt of lightning. The rose-colored glasses disappeared, and for the very first time I finally connected with what being black and a nigger meant. I don't remember crying or saying anything because I was stunned. What did all our years together mean? When I was younger, her mother would stroke my hair and smile, and say something in Ukrainian, which I never understood but I always took to be complimentary – now I wondered. I was mad, not at her parents, but at my lifelong friend for not sticking up for me, for not challenging her parents' prejudice. Why wasn't I good enough to sleep at their house? Did they think my color would rub off on them? Did I stink? I never told my parents what had happened. My life took a 180-degree turn that day. From then on, I started to wonder if there could truly be a true friendship between people of different races.

Some weeks later, I was waiting for the bus at Runnymede station with four male schoolmates following a track and field event. I had come first in every event I had entered. One of the guys asked, "What do you want to be when you grow up?" "J" wanted to be a doctor so he could look at naked women. "R" wanted to be an engineer, "G" an architect, and "F" wanted to work in the foreign service as a diplomat. And then all eyes fell on me. "What do you want to be, Jasmine?" When I explained that I wanted to be a teacher, they all broke down laughing and "J" took the extra step of rolling on the ground, just to make a point. And finally, "R" blurted out through his laughter, "Well, if you are going to be a teacher then I am going to be the president of the United States." I rode home in silence, the boys still giggling and jabbing each other about my ridiculous dream of becoming a teacher. I was puzzled. My marks were better than all of theirs. I was a straight A student in Grade Six. Why did they feel I was incapable of becoming a teacher? As the years passed, I started to pay attention to who my teachers were, who the principals were, and then it began to dawn on me. I had never seen, nor had been taught by a black person. Maybe I couldn't be a teacher. Maybe black people were not smart enough. My self-esteem plummeted.

A short time after, the gym teacher, who looked like a member of Air Supply with his strawberry blond, shoulder-length hair, coiffed and feathered perfectly, and his sunburned freckled skin, had us sitting in a circle in the hall as we waited for our chartered bus to take us to another track meet. He started going around the circle asking people various questions like "Where are you from?" His finger landed on me. I responded that I was born in England. He waved his hand back and forth impatiently as if to erase writing on a blackboard and said, "No, no. There are no black people in England. Where are your parents from?" This would become a familiar refrain I would hear time and time again throughout my adult years.

In Grade Seven, I was put in a split 7/8 class with five other Grade Sevens. We were all friends and excellent students. I missed a lot of class due to volleyball, basketball, track and field, cross-country and the odd drama practice. But I never let my school work slip. I was very shy. And being in a class with girls with Dolly Parton breasts and boys with beards was very unnerving. All of the Grade Sevens scored relatively the same on tests and were very competitive. So when I received my report card, I was very shocked to see that I had received D's in Math, Reading, and Science. I was devastated. I had never received anything lower than a B+. I was really puzzled. At parent-teacher night, my teacher suggested to my mom that I should be kept back a year and that my parents should consider sending me to a technical high school to learn typing so that I could move right into being a secretary after Grade Thirteen. My teacher had already shipped me off to technical school in her mind. The colonial mindset had taught my mother never to question a teacher's "good counsel." It was my older sister who reminded my mom that I had just left Grade Six with straight A's, that clearly something was not right, and she should fight to see that I was put ahead. So the teacher reluctantly passed me on to Grade Eight. From that day on I wanted nothing to do with typing (I still can't type). I also decided that my sports and extracurricular activities would have to be curtailed significantly. I remained captain of the volleyball and basketball teams but pulled out of many track and field sports, even when the principal and gym teacher tried to convince my parents to send me to run professionally. I refused. I was a gifted athlete but sports were not my first love. I didn't want to be known as a jock; I wanted to be educated – well-educated. I wanted to prove to those boys and myself that I could be a teacher.

My younger sister and I took piano lessons after school and one day in Grade Eight, as we were leaving the schoolyard an hour past the end of school, my lifelong tormentor lay in wait for us with his even more delinquent brother. As we made our way across the expansive yard, they appeared from out of nowhere wielding a jackknife, jabbing it in our faces, waving it menacingly, threatening to cut our "fucking nigger throats." This is where I put my track skills to the test. I told my sister I would get help and sprinted past the boys with my sister running behind me. The two boys chased us screaming, "Nigger, you're dead!" I ran into traffic to escape them and sprinted for my life. As fate would have it, my mom was on her way home on the bus, riding by the school at that exact moment. She was standing up getting ready to disembark at the next stop but got off one stop earlier when she noticed that we were being chased by two boys. I literally ran into the arms of my mom, almost knocking her down. When the boys realized we knew her, they took off. We told our mother what had happened and she walked back to the school with us to speak to the principal, who was all too willing to give her the boys' home phone number and address. I don't know what my parents said to their parents but the taunting stopped. Even today I wonder what these boys might have done if they had caught us. Would they have slit our throats? Why did they hate us so much? Was the color of my skin so revolting?

In Grade Eight I studied every day. I became so nervous – to the point of nausea – about taking tests because I felt they would reveal that I wasn't good enough – that black people were stupid. After all, I had almost failed Grade Seven. I remember our first geography test. I rewrote my notes several times, memorizing the definitions in bold print from our textbook. And to my delight, our test was made up mostly of the bold words so I easily completed the test. I knew I had a perfect or close-to-perfect score. I was so relieved and convinced that things would fall back in order. Until the next day when the teacher called me to his desk. He handed me my paper which had a big red zero at the top and he scolded me for cheating on the test. He didn't allow me to speak so that I could explain why my answers were exact descriptions as found in the book. His logic was ridiculous because I sat at a desk attached to his with five other students. Surely if I had cheated, he would have seen me. The lesson I learned that day was, I better not do too well on tests and assignments because the teacher would never believe it was my own work and thus accuse me of cheating.

At the beginning of track season, I proceeded to the gym to sign up for one or two events only to find that the gym teacher had signed me up for several more. I was furious but too shy to complain. I complained bitterly to my friend. She went directly to our home room teacher to explain the problem. I was so surprised that he took me with him in tow to see the gym teacher to demand that I be removed from the events I hadn't picked. That was the first time in seven years that I had decided to only do two track events – the 50-yard dash and relay. The gym teacher wasn't pleased and the way she showed it was by giving me a D in gym. But just to make her point, at graduation, the Athlete of the Year Award was given to a girl who had just come to the school the year before. Several teachers approached the gym teacher at graduation to inquire why I didn't get the award. The gym teacher came up to me and whispered in my ear with a smirk on her face, "If you had been more cooperative it could have been yours." There were no tears, just the sad realization that life was not fair.

As a young child, I never contemplated the color of my skin and the many barriers I would have to overcome because of it. My parents never told me, "Look, people are going to treat you differently because your skin is darker than theirs," or that people would challenge my intellectual ability, believing that I was only good for sports and dancing.

It makes me sad that the wonderful memories of my childhood will always be tainted by the actions of a few people. Today, I look back at the many incidents that could have knocked my life onto another trajectory, but it didn't happen because of the good people – family and friends – who helped me overcome setbacks and regain my faith in people. I learned to navigate systems that fail to acknowledge racial inequality in their practices and policies. Above all, I know that those experiences shaped my character, built my resolve to go after my goals in life, knowing that I can attain them. I am what I am today because I believed in myself.

Compiled by Anita Sechesky

Jasmine Jackman is the President of the United Nations Association Regional Toronto Branch, the regional director of the National Association of Multicultural Educators-NAME, and an award nominated educator, mentor teacher, and social justice advocate. She has worked with underserved youth in the Greater Toronto Area since 1980. She has chaired both professional and community diversity/equity committees, and sits on the board of the United Nations Association of Canada Toronto Region, Skills for Change, Bridging the Gap, and the African Women's Acting Association. Jasmine is a doctoral candidate at OISE/University of Toronto in Educational Policy and Leadership.

Compiled by Anita Sechesky

Diamond Glitters of Self-Healing

"A woman needs to accept herself for the beautiful gem she is, both outside and inside. There is no one else like her and that's why she is a rare and precious person of priceless value. The more that a woman chooses to accept and acknowledge this within her life, the more healing is released into her soul."

~ Anita Sechesky

Leah Lucas

Diamond Letters

Dear Diamond Sisters;

This is my purpose, my life, my loves. One who is passed but guiding me by light and love from above. That woman is my mother. One far away but yet closer to my heart more now then ever. That woman is my sister. The two I love the most, the deepest, and hold most dear. They are my treasure. These two, that I hold as often and as tight as they will allow me too. These are my two children. My soul. My life. My everything. These precious gifts in life are what allow me to breath life every single day. I am nothing without these precious things. Plus a few others. They know how much they mean to me also.

We all fight our own battles from within. Struggling to see the truth from behind the high tides life can brings us. What is real? What is hiding beneath the surface? How do we know which direction to go? Are we gonna be alright? What if we get lost? Who's there to lead the way?

Well, truth is, we don't know. We don't know what tomorrow holds. This, this is called the "journey." We all have one. All our own.

It's why we are here. Why we exist. To journey, to live these fears and learn how to continue on our journey till the end…whatever way that may take you. It's you're journey. It's your life. What will you choose? Where will you travel? How far will you go? Who will you take with you? Or will you walk alone? It's a mystery this journey.

You know that feeling? The one that scares you and makes it hard to breath. That's the fear inside us that we all have. It's meant to feel scary uncomfortable. We want to avoid it. We can't. Why? Well, it serves a purpose to move us through the highest tides. Forces waves of change in our lives to be able to reach further into the distance beyond. We need fear to survive. Without it, there's really nothing to fight for is there? I don't think so. That's just me though.

Tsunami's are inevitable. So powerful in force to where we feel as if we are sinking into the crashing waves, getting trapped by debris, and taken into the deepest darkest of places but somehow as we struggle and fight to survive, something catches our eyes and we stretch out and pull ourselves to the surface once more. Is it a light? A vision in our darkest hour of hope? A simple thought of someone we love? What do you see that gives you reason to just hang on longer?

We almost sink. We want to give into the void. Yet, we don't. Why? What did we see that gave us that last deepest breath we may have ever breathed as of yet in life? The last of our energy we pull from deep within ourselves that keeps us above the surface. What is it? I call that "purpose." My purpose is bright and it shines as far as my eyes can see. I see my precious gifts. That's all I need is those gifts to continue the battle onward.

In life, we try and break through the waves, surf where we can, and enjoy that ride while we can. The sun shines; happiness is all around. Our journey is life and we are living it to the fullest.

However, nothing is ever promised in life. Nothing worth having ever comes easy. I know this. You know this. Our journey continues and we all walk the path till we arrive, wherever that may be. That's yet to be found. At the finish, at the end of our journey, you will know.

I'm not perfect, I don't wanna be. I'm not a princess, though a guy I know makes me feel like one even on my very worst of days. I struggle and fight my fight from within. I battle my demons. I walk my journey. I walk with God close by. I invite others into my life that bring light and love and happiness that makes me want to shine brighter and be as strong as I can be. I also invite people into my life to help teach me lessons along the way. These people's journey may bring road blocks. Paths to dangers that seek out ways to distract me from my goal to reach the end of my journey peacefully and safe. I manage to travel my path although sometimes painful, almost too much to bare. I just keep going. I have my precious gifts and my purpose. Until I reach my end, that's where I'll be.

What will your journey be? Where will you go? Or where will you allow your journey to take you? High or low? Whatever you chose, is what will be.

Find your reason, your hope, your light, or precious gifts. Enjoy each day. Be present.

As the saying goes: "Yesterday is history, tomorrow is a mystery, today is a gift which is why we call it the present."

Compiled by Anita Sechesky

Stephanie Roy

Chapter 4

Rough Cuts

As the legends go, a diamond is not born a precious gem, but begins as a plain piece of coal. Only with time, polish, and yes, the occasional scrapes from the elements, does it become the priceless object it is. Technically, this is not really true, but let's say it is for the sake of metaphor. My point is, we don't just become strong, loving, and caring individuals by accident. It is a long, arduous process through bad times, good times, and experience to become who we are.

For anyone else who has had the occasional "nature vs nurture" debate with some random guy in a bar, you know what I'm talking about. Although nature definitely plays some part, the majority of our personalities come from what we experience in our lifetime, the good and the bad.

Friends are the people we choose to compliment our lives. I've been blessed throughout my life to have the best friends in the world. I have met them in many various times and places one would never expect. It has been my experience that the best friends are the ones you go through the worst experiences with.

"J" would have to be the friend I have known the longest. We met in kindergarten and have been best friends ever since. Maybe we were close because we were the class nerds. I used to be super tall, awkward, and weird; she was short with glasses and braces. We both got good grades so that might have helped. "Sports are for stupid people," we used to say since that was how we would justify the fact that we were terrible at everything athletic. We were bullied and harassed a lot because of our lack of athletic expertise, but we discovered over time that there was strength in numbers.

We eventually started recruiting others who were ostracised for whatever reason; being shy, weird, short, tall, rich, poor, skinny, fat, etc. We were the "nerds club" who would sit outside on the edge of the baseball field in what we called "the nest" which was a pile of branches and twigs we pulled around us which did indeed look like a nest. There were usually a group of three to seven depending on who was there. We always encouraged anyone to join, and sometimes even a few of the popular kids would come by to check out what we were up to. Then we would do whatever we wanted... read, write, draw, talk about weird subjects...all without judgment. I didn't realize it then, but we created a place where we could safely explore our own natural abilities. It was there where I wrote my first short story. I even wrote the idea for a Christmas play which is still used by the grade eight class there to this day. I was so shy at the time I was afraid to give my ideas to the teacher, but "J" convinced me to or she would do it herself. She also taught me to stand up for myself. I guess being bullied actually did make us stronger.

We stayed friends even after elementary school when she moved to a different city with her family. I missed her terribly during high school and refused to make new friends. I had a few friends but it was never the same. We called each other on the phone and even wrote letters once in a while. When we grew up we both got married, and yes, we were in each other's wedding parties. As adults, a whole new set of problems was discovered. We supported each other through infidelities, spousal abuse, child abuse, mental health problems, child-rearing issues, and deaths in our families. All this made us stronger because we knew someone was there for each other no matter what. This is why friends are so important – they help each other grow to their full potential without judgment.

Another important friend in my life was "T." I was living in a city where the only person I knew was my abusive boyfriend. After a botched kidnapping incident, and a fight with a security guard at the Greyhound bus station, I ended up at a women's shelter. I thankfully never saw him again. This is where I met "T", the sweetest most positive and loving person I have ever met. If my life sounded bad, you can't imagine the horror show this girl's life was and what led her there. It made me realize not to be sad if I couldn't afford a pair of shoes because someone else had no feet. At the time, I had so much rage and negativity towards the man who caused me to end up in that shelter, but when I heard her story, I could not understand how she didn't have as much hate in her heart as me. Even after getting attacked one night in the shelter and having her nose broken by some other girl in there, "T" had nothing but forgiveness and peace in her heart. When I asked her why, she told me it would otherwise poison her. I learned a lot in that shelter – men were not the only enemy, and to embrace forgiveness for those who have wronged you. Life is too short to be on their level, and in the end, if you become hateful like them, they've won.

There was another dark time in my life when I met "H." We were both involved with men who were in very dangerous lifestyles, which meant we were involved as well. It was a situation where two innocent girls like ourselves were forced to become strong mentally to survive. There were times when we wanted to break down and cry but we kept each other strong by becoming close friends. Having a twisted sense of humor was also helpful. In the end, we were both able to get out of that lifestyle and move in together in another town. I introduced her to an old friend and they instantly fell in love. That was ten years ago. I will be at their wedding next year and I couldn't be happier. She has a great husband (to be) with a normal job, three beautiful kids, and the white picket fence lifestyle that she always wanted. Together, we learned to never regret anything or avoid shady situations because you never know what you will learn, and in the end, it did make us both stronger and able to take on anything without fear. Besides, that life wasn't all that bad, it just would have been if we had stayed any longer. Always know when to leave.

You know that cliché about how when one door closes, another one opens? That's pretty much what happened with my friend "E." After moving to yet another city, I found myself alone once again after being betrayed and abandoned by another friend. "A" and I had moved to this city together with hopes and dreams, but when my sister got terminally ill, "A" decided my life was too much of a burden for him and he left me not only friendless, but homeless. Just when I was thinking I would never find a place to live, I had a dog and no job, I wandered down to the dock by our place. This is where I met "E", the kindest, most eccentric girl I have ever met. Funny thing is, she was looking for a roommate.

Not only did she offer me, a complete stranger and her dog, a place to live, she became another of my most trusted friends ever. While living together as roommates that year, my sister passed away. I was afraid to unburden my feelings on her after what happened with "A" but she encouraged it. The night before I left for a month to spend those last moments with my sister, "E" set up a mini Christmas holiday party. She knew how much I loved Christmas, and since I was leaving in December, she knew I would not exactly be having the best holiday ever. Her dad came with his guitar and we sang Christmas carols all night. It was a beautiful feeling that I didn't realize I needed at that moment. I guess she always understood that about me; most people can be consoled with hugs and sympathetic platitudes. She knew that a kind deed and a smile was what I needed, not tears. When her father passed away, I dropped everything to come to her place with a bottle of wine, food, and ears to listen to her. We've been through many ups and downs since then, and even though we are no longer roommates, we are still friends who support each other when needed. She taught me how important it is to stay positive no matter what the situation, and that your friends can be just as important as family when you live far away from home.

There is something to be said also of "good time friends" and "bad time friends." The former are the ones who are always there when there's a party or good time to be had, but when the s#&t really hits the fan, they're nowhere to be found. Then there's the latter who you may not see as often but when something happens, they're by your side without hesitation. Finally, there's that special breed of friend who is both. They are hard to find but when you are lucky enough to do so, hang onto them like a kid clutches a candy bar because they are precious.

There have been many other very important friends over the years, but there are too many painful and wonderful moments to put down on paper. That's right, the best friends are the ones you go through the best and worst moments of your life. Painful times are the true test of a friend's loyalty. And sometimes the people you least expect turn out to be the best ones. In life, we all find ourselves in a place where we are too weak to stand on our own. This is why good friends are important. Likewise, it is just as important to be that friend also. After all, we are all a mirror of the ones we meet.

Like attracts like. The bottom line is, you don't just "have" good friends, you earn them by being one.

After reading over what I've written, it's occurred to me that aside from the fact that my best friends come from different backgrounds and parts of the country, they all have one thing in common. They all have had mental issues and experienced hard times at certain periods of their lives. I guess I've always been attracted to like-minded individuals with intense personalities who are often misunderstood and rejected from the typical mainstream train of thought. To quote Jack Kerouac, a man who feels like a kindred spirit to me:

"[...]the only people for me are the mad ones, the ones who are mad to live, mad to talk, mad to be saved, desirous of everything at the same time, the ones who never yawn or say a commonplace thing, but burn, burn, burn like fabulous yellow roman candles exploding like spiders across the stars and in the middle you see the blue centerlight pop and everybody goes "Awww!"

— Jack Kerouac, On the Road

Stephanie Roy is an aspiring author who graduated from Algoma University in 2011 with a BA in Psychology and a Minor in English Literature. Her goal is to understand human nature and has been trying to accomplish this endeavor by being employed in as many different occupations as possible including taxi driver, carnival worker, actress, and youth worker in high risk areas. Stephanie currently resides in Montreal, Quebec with her dog Sadie, and is working on an autobiography about her sister who passed away from cancer, and the impact this disease leaves behind for families and loved ones.

https://www.facebook.com/stephanie.roy.735?ref=br_rs

Compiled by Anita Sechesky

Anita Sechesky

Chapter 5

A Woman's Spirit Is Her Strength

A woman's spirit is unbreakable and beautiful in so many ways. It allows the essence of a woman to be connected to her human mind and body, and it has the ability to connect with other human beings, both men and women alike. The differences I have witnessed and experienced for myself as a woman is the unlimited ability to be empathetic and open to loving others in such a way that your soul feels embodied of so many emotions and incumbent thoughts that flood your preconceived thought patterns to switch from that of general awareness to that of survival mode.

In our physical ability to be the future creators of life, we walk with an awareness that cannot be put into words but can only be experienced through reality or a deep emotional connection to the individual or having lived a similar experience of your own. This ability I believe comes from the physiological programming to create life within the female body. It is through this same process a woman also has the experience of learning and adapting to human death such as the loss of a pregnancy or stillbirth through the degeneration of living cells within the same womb that was bringing a life together. It is through this symbiotic state I also feel that the female spirit is different than that of a male. As women, we have the ability to tap into this physiological process through our spiritual state of awareness and of course because our cells' DNA do not forget the imprint of that experience. Science has already proven that our cells have memory. We can experience deep emotional pain or trauma another person has lived through, based on our own lived experiences and shared memories from anyone else who may have triggered a connection. I believe that love is such a powerful energy that it causes our spirits to become linked as one. I am also a strong believer that our spirits live forever.

I would like to share my own personal experience when I had lost my first child. My daughter was full-term and she was a perfect baby. But, first I would like to share something that as a Registered Nurse for many years, working in various hospitals and Nursing homes, I have heard various stories from colleagues and patients over the years about Angels that have been known to bring comfort and inspiration to those who believe. Despite the ordeal of losing our first child, I still feel I was very blessed to have my own Angel and spiritual experience during and after the loss of my beautiful baby daughter, Jasmine Rose, who was full-term and born sleeping. It was a tough time for me and I had gone through a period where it was next to impossible to even talk about it. I couldn't even pray and asked my husband and mom to pray on my behalf as my heart was filled with so much grief and anxiety. I had completely lost my self-expression to inconsolable tears and heartache as her death was so unexpected. As the weeks went by, the crying changed to fear and then to nightmares.

A week or so after our daughter's burial, I started having very disturbing dreams that left me terrified and feeling even more helpless and isolated. One particular night, I was sitting up in bed reading, and out of the "corner of my eye," I got glimpse of something that has completely changed my perspective on supernatural beings. I witnessed the most astounding sight – right in front of me in full view for that brief second. It was like a multidimensional experience. I saw the biggest, most beautiful, and lushest wings that were swooping down across the bedroom floor, the feathers were of the hugest plumes I have ever seen. I saw arms, the biggest arms with muscles that were formed, flexed, folded across, and very developed, and a strong male chest. I saw a Roman skirt with long leather pleats. I saw the leather sandals that were laced up two very strong legs. I saw the sword that was strapped across the chest and hanging to the left side of his body. The blade on the sword was huge and heavy. And then I saw the face of this Angel man. He had the face of a baby, just like a cherub, gentle but yet stern. The look on his face was serious and he was on guard at the end of my bedroom, guarding me. My world instantly shifted to understand that I was not alone in this journey. God really did care for me and He sent his very best to protect and watch over me, despite how fearful I may have been feeling. I never did have another bad dream again after that night.

Looking back, there was nothing wrong my entire pregnancy and this is what has been the biggest struggle to overcome – the releasing of what was done wrong as it can never be made right in this life. We did lose our beautiful little girl due to unforeseen causes that were quite preventable had certain professionals done their jobs properly. I had known something was not right and felt it within my heart the moment things began to stir up in my spirit. I asked my doctor if I could be induced to have my daughter delivered two weeks early. My Obstetrician's office was over two hours away from my hometown. He decided not to interfere with the natural birth process that was planned since there wasn't any cause for concern at this point. When I went to the Emergency Department in my small hometown in Northwestern, Ontario, I was always told by the nurses that everything was fine even though my baby's heart rate was lower as compared to earlier assessments in my pregnancy. Although this experience occurred before I became a Registered Nurse, it did not sit well within my soul and actually left me quite disturbed as I already had some medical knowledge and computers were providing much fingertip knowledge at the time.

This first pregnancy loss with my daughter was the most heartbreaking thing I can honestly say that I have endured in life. No one from my hometown hospital offered any support, my church family did their one week of follow up duty to provide a meal every day. No counseling was offered by my church or community. My doctor told me at a follow-up appointment that I should start a support group, instead of offering any support. The rather large corporation, that my husband worker for did not offer any employee assistance support to a grieving father or mother. Looking back, it appears, in my professional opinion as a Certified Professional Coach and Specialized RN, that everyone expected us to have all the answers to our situation and that our problem was just that – our problem. It saddens me to think that a whole community could not see how important any loss of life is and how, little by little, it tears away at the fabric of society if no one cares. You see, every life is precious and every spirit born and released through death has a purpose. It is up to the living left behind to realize that eventually there is accountability in some way and in some dimension of time and reality as we may or may not know it. In hindsight, I realize that I entered into a season of Post-Traumatic Stress Disorder. I had no professional support, as my small hometown community did not have a support group in place, although my Physician encouraged me to start a special group for other grieving parents.

My hometown had a number of families who had also suffered similar tragedies. Obviously, I was not ready at this time of my life to take on such a responsibility; I myself was walking through this horrific ordeal as well. My husband dealt with his grief quietly, although he was very supportive to me. After all, how can grieving parents start a support group if they no support to begin with? How good is a medical professional when there is no form of accountability? What about a community of individuals who gossip, whisper, and yet offer no kind words, support, hugs, and prayers? Many pockets of society have communities that suffer this same fate of neglect regardless of how big or small. Many communities are dealing with serious issues of suicides, abuse, and homelessness of children, yet no one is stepping up to address the human spirt that is suffering through it all. No one is attempting to speak up and call it out for what it is. Many people know and would rather stay out of it. They don't want to be associated, yet they feel comfortable gossiping and spreading hurtful rumors. This is a scourge that has gotten out of control in our world today. This is an epidemic that is hurting the human spirit that wants to thrive and needs love to live without the limitations of everything negative. Until we choose to see what is fragmenting the human spirit through our own actions and inactions, we cannot help one another to build a better world for the future generations. Ignorance is not always bliss, it can actually be destructive in more ways than we may care to realize. If more women recognized that as women, regardless of who we are and where we come from, we do go through many similarities and when our children hurt, our world hurts. There would be so much healing taking place, it could begin to change the hearts of many nations.

Sadly, the loss of my baby girl was not the first one in this beautiful community. I tried to tell the nurses so many times that something was not right, but yet no one took me seriously. Not once did my doctor get called in, considering I was full-term and due at any minute. I must have gone to the Emergency Department at least a dozen times and was always told that I was over thinking or something to that extent. The last time I went to Emerg, they staff finally took me seriously and put a stress monitor on me. All the previous times I went in, the stress monitor was being used or I was just sent home. I wasn't even given the option to wait for the monitor for a short duration to confirm any of my concerns. In fact, this last visit to the emergency room, gave me the information that I should go into my doctor's office tomorrow, not a "HOLD ON"…I'm going to call your doctor in, OR we are going to fly you into Thunder Bay…Nope…Not at all. Imagine the accountability that someone will have one day. I am strong believer that sometimes, when people do not like you, they will not make any effort for you. Hate has never saved a soul. Enough said.

As it turned out, my precious baby girl was stillborn, two days later and I had to deliver her in a maternity ward during the Christmas holidays just two days before my own birthday. It was heart-wrenchingly painful to see the other mothers and their beautiful precious living bundles of joy. I will never forget the looks I was given when I was encouraged to go for a walk and as I walked into the common room, I knew they knew I had lost my Jasmine Rose. The sad and empty looks from the other parents was something that cannot be put into words. I got up quickly and left the room as I did not want to make them feel uncomfortable.

The night before my induction, my baby daughter's glimmering and translucent spirit came to me and before I knew it, I was hovering above my body looking down at my husband lying next to my own lifeless body. I saw how my hands were folded across my pregnant belly with my daughter's fetal body still within my womb. I remember lovingly gazing at her with curiosity and taking in how beautiful and bright she was and then, just like that, I got caught up in the instantaneous rapture of leaving my physical body. In the instance that I was traveling upwards into the heavenly realms with my daughter, I remembered what my mom had just moments earlier spoken to me about and I looked back down at my husband sleeping. She said that I should remember how much he loved me and that we would have more children one day. The very moment that incredible thought flashed through my mind, I was back inside my physical body but this time, once again looking at my hands folded in front of me across my bulging belly. Can you believe that my doctor never gave my husband and I any clue something was wrong? We packed our vehicle with our baby car seat, our baby homecoming clothes and diapers, and extra blankets…can you imagine the numbness of what it was like to leave the hospital to go our daughter's funeral with an empty baby car seat behind me? There are no words, even now after all these years. No words of what it was like to look in the mirror and see her eyes on me, her eyebrows on me…unless you have experienced it you will not even understand what I just said.

This spiritual experience left me realizing that death is only a transition with no physical effort at all. In fact, my experience was completely effortless and merely a shift out of my physical body and fully aware of my spiritual body. I guess you can say it's no different than getting undressed. I believe that we already have our spiritual bodies inside of us and when we no longer need our physical bodies, we simply leave them behind in the physical world.

However you may want to analyze it, this I can say was a profound and powerful revelation that gave me confirmation of life after death. How amazing to know that we never actually die or lose ourselves but we are intact in our thoughts even after our physical bodies stop working! This is why I am a strong believer in my Christian faith. I choose to believe that I will be reunited with my loved ones and even embrace my baby girl once more in my arms.

I have learned that our spirit man or woman is the essence of exactly who we are. This concept is so profound that it can help us to become stronger in this life if we allow ourselves to accept that nothing is impossible and that all is possible if we believe. Many women find an almost supernatural strength they never knew existed within themselves when they are going through the worst of times in their lives. It is through these lived experiences we become stronger in this life.

Yes, the human spirit is powerful and I can even tell you an experience I had with one of my pets. When our dear family pet died, it was a hard time for all of us as our doggie girl was part of our family for over thirteen years. She was like our first child and she was well loved within our community by our friends and family. I will never forget that following the first Mother's Day service after we had lost our daughter, our pet doggie came into the bedroom and looked at me as I was curled up on my bed crying. She jumped up and snuggled right against my belly, as if someone had coaxed her to do that. She stayed there for a brief moment, jumped down, looked at me, and then walked away. When our beloved pet passed away at my parent's home, it was devastating because we never had a chance to say good-bye to her. The following day, I was sitting in my glider rocking chair just thinking that I never had a chance to tell her how much I loved her. All of a sudden, out of nowhere, I literally felt this amazing rush of energy. It was like a swift breeze. Before I knew it, our dog in her spiritual form was sitting right next to me by my feet. Then automatically I felt my Spirit man lean down, pat her, and even say, "Good girl." I couldn't believe this was happening and excitedly told my husband that I got to say goodbye to our pet. He was so happy and never doubted me because of the supernatural experiences I already had.

My reason for sharing these events is to help you realize that our spirit is something that we all contain within us. There is no explaining it. I believe from the time our cells are conceived and start vibrating, we are created out of pure love and positive energy as we are all perfect creations by God within this Universe and all its glory. There is no need to fear the fact that our spirit is something that is unexplained. In fact, I believe in some special way, if we embrace our lives differently we may be exposed to more infinite possibilities that we would never have realized were always around us anyways. Many people already know that God is a spirit as we cannot see Him, yet we believe He exists around us. Be open-minded to what our Creator has created within you. You are unique and wonderfully made. Never doubt the endless possibilities of your human spirit. This life is but a journey and we are all headed in the same direction.

As you already know, this book is to help you see how we are all connected. We don't have to personally know each other to understand life's hardships, trauma, and pain. Our unity as individuals simply believing in the common good creates a connection within our spirits. Can you imagine so many people across the globe equally realizing the need to reach out and show more empathy, compassion, and love for those around them? The human spirit ignited in love will unite many and it will all be for the greater good. God is Love. Have you connected with Him as yet? It's all about relationship, not rituals. Just like any other relationship, start with introducing yourself. He accepts you just as you are. Maybe it's time you do the same. Healing will become one of the benefits from this relationship. It all starts with you wanting more for yourself. The human spirit is one of the most beautiful gifts we have been given. It has unlimited possibilities. It took me almost ten full years to talk about the loss of my daughter Jasmine Rose, without becoming emotional. It's still a sting and still an empty void. I now understand why I have always felt this way even though my husband and I have two beautiful boys today. It's because each person has a soul and a purpose. Each living person has a personality, No one can ever be replaced, just as we have the ability to love all of our children and family. Each connection is unique and with a special bond.

Many times in life, we may face extreme difficulties in our lives that leave us questioning our soul purpose. There is no reason to be hard on yourself if you don't have it all figured out today. Don't ever lose hope in who you are – searching inside your heart and soul will give you direction to begin your inward and outward journey to self, regardless of whether you see how powerful and special you are today. One day you will see the reason you have never given up and are drawn to strong women and encourage others. You have a beautiful spirit that wants to help you live your life with so much joy and unlimited love. Not everyone may be supportive in your journey but that doesn't mean you should give up on yourself. In fact, it means to never give up because that is where your true strength lives, within you! Lives are changed instantly as a result of either good or bad experiences. When you carry pain deep within your heart, it affects the vibrancy of your life. As you are attracting more positive people, you feel yourself grow spiritually as the need to evolve is being nourished, being around like-minded individuals.

Healing has begun. Embrace it and watch your spirit soar as you fulfil your destiny in life by becoming everything loving you were created to be. I encourage you to continue discovering what your life's passions are by always searching deep within your soul.

Compiled by Anita Sechesky

Anita Sechesky is the Founder and CEO of Anita Sechesky - Living Without Limitations Inc. She is an RN, CPC, Best-Seller Publisher, Multiple International Best-Selling Author, as well as a Law of Attraction and NLPP.

Anita is also the CEO, Founder, Owner, and Publisher of her company LWL PUBLISHING HOUSE.

Currently she has successfully branded 300 International Best-Selling authors in the last three years. LWL PUBLISHING HOUSE is a division of her company, in which she offers coaching, mentoring, motivation, marketing, and of course publishing services for her clients. 2016 marks the addition of two new branches in LWL PUBLISHING HOUSE dedicated specifically to children's books of inspiration and learning, and also fiction and non-fictional single author books.

Working with Anita at one of her "LWL INSPIRED TO WRITE" workshops, Webinars or one-to-one support, will equip you to step out of your comfort zone fearlessly! Anita's solo book entitled "Absolutely You - Overcome False Limitations & Reach Your Full Potential" was written in less than four weeks and she can teach you how to do the same!

CEO of Anita Sechesky – Living Without Limitations Inc., Founder and Publisher of LWL PUBLISHING HOUSE.

Best-Seller Mentor, Book Writing Coach, Registered Nurse, Certified Professional Coach, Master NLPP and LOA Practitioner, multiple International Best-Selling Author, Workshop Facilitator & Trainer, Conference Host, Keynote Speaker.

Join my Private Facebook group: LIVING WITHOUT LIMITATIONS LIFESTYLE.

With over 960 members, we offer exclusive prizes, co-authoring opportunities, Random Contests with FREE Publishing possibilities, "Inspired to Write" Webinar classes, and more - http://bit.ly/1TlsTSm

Please visit our Facebook page: LWL PUBLISHING HOUSE

Website: www.lwlpublishinghouse.com

Email: lwlclienthelp@gmail.com.

Join my Private Facebook group:

LIVING WITHOUT LIMITATIONS LIFESTYLE: Exclusive prizes, co-authoring opportunities and Random Contests with FREE Publishing opportunities. http://bit.ly/1TlsTSm

YouTube Channel: http://bit.ly/1VEGHew

Website: www.anitasechesky.com

LinkedIn: https://ca.linkedin.com/in/asechesky

Twitter: https://twitter.com/nursie4u

Currently, we are filling co-author opportunities for all our upcoming #Hashtag

books in this series:

#Joy – *The Emotion to Embrace*

#Faith – *The Gift that Keeps on Giving*

Compiled by Anita Sechesky

Diana Alli D'Souza

Chapter 6

There is More to Life

Life is like a deck of cards: you never know whether you'll be dealt a good or bad hand. Depending on the player's luck, with a wild card in the mix, the game can sway to beat the odds, so much so that life has a way of rescuing us from catastrophes.

We all go through our ups and downs. Some are bombarded with never-ending storms, others like me have redirected the wind through a healing process with great support systems, loyal friends, self-determination, and a strategic planning process. It took me along the road less traveled with a richer, deeper, and vibrant purpose.

The loss through tragic deaths of my dad and brother just six months apart, my parents' failing marriage, my own disastrous marital breakup, single-parenthood and more: I identified these crazy stages of life as soul transformation; processing my diamond in the rough, metaphorically speaking, the fire and brilliance only uncovered after the cutting and polishing process.

My adolescent years were positive, memorable ones filled with fun, laughter, and camaraderie between loving extended family circles, and mischievous banter with my siblings, cousins, and friends.

Around my tenth birthday, my mother chose to leave what I had assumed was a strong nuclear family unit. This had a profound impact on me, and had emotional consequences in piecing together my fragmented soul. In the early '60s, divorce was a misdemeanor; this sudden separation drew much public attention in a diverse faith-based community in Mumbai, India. Marriage was then considered sacred. Many relationships survived against all odds.

My parental break-up took an immense toll on my emotional development provoking me through my trying stages of puberty and subsequent adulthood. It was later on that I began to piece together the false sense of well-being, reassuring myself that all would work out.

I was a pro at the fight or flight syndrome, habitually running away from one frying pan into the next fire. Using travel as a band aid, I whisked to chase the winds from India, to the UK, to Canada – from one home to the next. I preferred to be alone in this maze of despair.

I married the first handsome young man I met, hoping he would be my lifelong partner; it soon turned sour, violent, and abusive. My life was falling apart. I held onto my crumbling marriage like a martyr, letting emotional turmoil fill me with ammunition of self-pity. As long as I could remember, I was a people pleaser; acquiescing to other people's needs and desires, in and out of one abusive relationship to the next, somehow meeting insecure men with their own baggage weighing them down.

I looked up to God with the usual excuse, "Why me Lord?" Why did life treat me so unkindly? I was nothing but a victim of my past. Now I too was ridden with shame, guilt, resentment, and regret. Thankfully I sought appropriate therapy and so did my kids. I took my innocent children out of the abusive home. After all, I was as much to blame if I continued to let my kids witness their mother going through hell; I was an enabler so to speak.

Thanks to the health care institution I worked at, folks saw my external wounds, gauged my internal despair, and urged me to get out. It was a blessing in disguise. Today my children, all married with their bundles of joy aged from seven to the early twenties, are stronger, confident, and resilient. With mending mind, soul, and body, I was able to be a stronger influence in their lives.

It took years to reshape my emotional thought pattern, but I now believe that no matter where you've been and no matter how badly life treated you, there is always a way out. Carl Jung said, "Who looks outside, dreams, who looks inside, awakes…when we look outside, our true heart awakes." I realized then that I needed to reframe my vision, reignite my passion and purpose in life. A good start was to begin by honoring me, making a commitment to me. I had to give up on all the pointless drama, all the toxic relations that followed me, focusing on new horizons, trusting in myself for my life to go through the process of transformation and empowerment. I had to face my own demons, reassuring myself that tough times never last, but tough people do. I chose a purpose of finding me. Life had not forgotten me, but experiences taught me to refocus my energy on turning my wounds into wisdom and my difficulties into opportunities.

I made a commitment to myself, a mantra that took control. I promised to work on lovingly accepting all my flaws and imperfections, pledging to make the best out of experiences life sent my way, whether good or bad, and to make every moment count. I soon began letting go of all my toxic thoughts and self-defeating expectations, behaviors, and people that were holding me back in life. Something in me awakened, as if a force bigger and more powerful than me took over my life, a guiding light that kept me safe and protected at all times. I forgave myself. I took charge of the next stages of my journey; no more excuses. I began to excel in both my personal and professional life. This cathartic process took on new meaning and purpose.

Peter Marshall emphasizes, "When we long for life without difficulties, remind us that oaks grow strong in contrary winds and diamonds are made under pressure." I accepted the fact that I was a diamond in the rough, friction necessary; the polish would soon sparkle its shine on me.

I was generally a forgiving person; it was a sacred foundation inscribed in my Catholic/Christian upbringing. I was forever reminded by my parents, by nuns at the convent school I attended, to forgive not seven times seven, but seventy times seven (Mathew:18-22); a command to forgive without limit! Although I was never provoked that often in a day or week, the enormity of so much junk dumped on my well-being was too overwhelming to bear. I strongly believe in daily acts of kindness. I learned over time that forgiveness is the most important factor to living with the prospects of peace and harmony. And so began my healing and restoration process; driving out of a painful strife to a new joy-filled life within me. I was the diamond in the rough; inspired by its meaning that a diamond is made from a common chunk of coal, not worth much of anything except for the fire. Only if a tremendous amount of pressure is applied, can coal become a diamond. I was made from God. Like a diamond, tension was applied testing my conviction and discipline, giving a chance to turn my fate around. As we look at one another, we appear common and ordinary, but I am a strong believer that God sees something precious in each one of us. The immense pressure is part of the process of making a diamond in the rough, ready to shine!

Over time I learned to let go. I needed to be able to forgive, but there were too many scars that embittered my soul. It took time, but I did find solace in making amends with my past. I realized that it does not mean that the past is easily erased; it certainly took me to a better place. The mighty warrior in me fastened my belt to take control of the fight in me, an astute trooper and activist, seizing every opportunity to empower others. I began to help women and girls who were exposed to all sort of violence, ensuring zero tolerance to any type of abuse. I reframed my fears into positive outcomes, challenging negative thoughts into great possibilities instead of being paralyzed by negative instincts. I am now fueled with strength and hope, ready to embrace uncertainties and cope better with the catastrophes that come my way.

I realized risk is necessary for growth, and perceived failures are part of that strange experience we call life. I began to focus on the possibilities instead of fear; the world will open up new opportunities. As I began to honor me, look at myself in the mirror and accept my own friendship first with me and then like-minded souls, my personal and professional journey began to carve out new paths and open new horizons. I now celebrate life, forceful with strong convictions. I allowed myself to be refined through the trials and tribulations life gifted me with.

In the late 1980s, with the overwhelming nature of medical school combined with personal stressors, we faced a number of suicides, finally grappling with three suicides in one that devastated the whole institution. Through recommendations from an accreditation process, I was tasked along with key leaders to start a centre enhancing student life and well-being. I was chosen to facilitate extracurricular opportunities threading in altruism and the humanitarian spirit. I identify this as Divine Intervention, transforming my journey, revaluating the institution's mission and purpose, and under God's masterful guiding light, I too was given a second chance to reflect and redefine my own framework, the true meaning and purpose life had in store for me.

With a compassionate and caring heart, my compass was reset. I soon became a pioneer and co-founder of over twenty-one outreach initiatives, some of which include:

- Benefit musical/dance performance concerts that raised tens of thousand dollars for destitute children and families around the world.

- Local initiatives serving the most marginalized, underrepresented populations in Toronto.

- Tutoring programs helping kids at risk of failing.

- Mentoring initiative for underrepresented students from Aboriginal and Black ancestry.

- Nurturing and supporting run-away moms and their children.

- Combatting homelessness including starting an interdisciplinary student-run clinic.

- Making a difference to children with disabilities and isolated seniors.

The list goes on with ongoing local and international recognition. I see these as miracles from above, blessed with earning meritorious accolades and distinguished honors and awards. Four years ago, I started www.accessempowermentcouncil.org serving the most destitute around the Globe, with my new found passion: teaching the most marginalized indigenous children.

Who would have thought I would lead, and not be led. I realized that when adversity stormed my way, gratitude had the power to bring hope; it is the key to growth and fulfilment. In the face of brokenness, forgiveness had the power to heal. When disaster robbed me of joy, faith positively intruded into my valuing life in its entirety. When faith at times is tested, I trust my intuition by paying full attention to the voice from God.

It has been a long journey. I now shift my worries to my higher being, knowing He is with me every step of the way. I do put humor into perspective, laughing at confusion and living consciously in the moment. Live and breathe this mantra, "You might not end up exactly where you intended to go, but you will eventually arrive precisely where you need to be." I am nearly there – my new way of thinking, faith, and hope being the central pillar of my distracted thoughts, letting go of the ghosts of past.

I now can relate to the most expensive gem of all; a "diamond" derived from the Greek word "adamas," which means invincible or indestructible. I am neither, but I am reassured that my gem is dazzling with shine. Had it not been for life's heart-wrenching moments, I would not have paid attention to the needs of gracing my soul with infinite love, forgiveness, and gratitude.

We were all born to be diamonds, going through the infinite process of being reshaped, revealing the brilliance within. I lucked out on the wild card put to good use, a win-win in the end after all. I know I have illuminated the world shining like a diamond.

A passionate trailblazer on Social Responsibility, Diana Alli D'souza has founded/co-founded and facilitated nationally recognized outreach programs in the Faculty of Medicine, University of Toronto. Through Utihp.ca she has raised tens of thousands of dollars for destitute children around the globe. Diana has served on numerous Boards: Governing Council, community foundations, local/national committees. She is the recipient of 12 MD graduation awards, University Awards, numerous University of Toronto awards, the prestigious Order of Ontario and the Queen Elizabeth II Diamond Jubilee Medal, and community recognition.

http://accessempowermentcouncil.org/our-team.html

Compiled by Anita Sechesky

Diamond Glitters of Joy

"A woman's joy should often be woven throughout her life like a precious jewel always surrounding her journey with beauty and grace. The people in her life should sense her great value by the gifts of laughter, happiness, and hope in all that she is and all that she contributes to."

~ *Anita Sechesky*

Compiled by Anita Sechesky

Winnie Smith

Diamond Letters

Dear Diamond Sisters;

I am writing to you to let you know that throughout this lifetime, when the floods are high and the tides are in, when you have no one to turn to, Your Abba father is waiting for you to call upon Him so that He can provide for you. He is your Jehovah Jireh, your provider, your protector, your portion and cup, your deliverer in every time of trouble. Your sustainer in every situation. Blessed are you, "my daughters you have done virtuously, and most of all excellent in God's eyes." It is a complete honor for me to write a salute to you all "my daughters of Zion, united in faith." Whether you are a spiritual daughter, or a natural daughter, you are blessed! I recall the lyrics of a beautifully written song, *"We are women, women of faith."* As soon as I heard this song, my heart was filled and I pondered on the lyrics, although the lyrics do not include "daughter," that is immediately where my heart was drawn to and I began mediating on the gift of motherhood of my spiritual children.

The gift of being a daughter can only be described by the word of faith. As a spiritual mother, I feel and carry the joy, the hurt, the triumph, and the disappointments of my spiritual daughters. I watch in awe as God molds and transforms you, yet somehow because of who He intended for you to be. As a natural mother, I prayerfully watch my daughters as they grow before God; I looked as they began to find their wings and began to soar with Him. Yet again somehow, it's never too much to bear. The reason for this is "Unshakable Faith." Without faith, one is like a stained glass, when the light cannot "Shine." I say this to you daughters of "Zion," *"For as the lightning cometh out of the east, and shineth even unto the west; so shall also the coming of the Son of man be"* **(Matthew 24:27) KJV.** "A bible with no context can be trouble." It is focused on the identity and the character of Jesus Christ.

There are many pictures of Jesus, but the word of God speaks volumes. God has said in His word *"And shall put my spirit in you, and ye shall live, and I shall place you in your own land: then shall ye know that I the LORD have spoken it, and performed it, saith the LORD"* **(Ezekiel 37:14) KJV.** Have you ever asked yourself, "What difference am I making with my life?" On some level, we all struggle to find our own answer to that fundamental question. The search for significance is the underlying motivation for virtually all human activity. It's what drives us. I want you to know that! A reasonable woman will continue to learn as long as she lives because life itself is a learning process. Any incident of life must have its lesson to teach us, for things don't just happen.

This is about a woman that was journeying on a one-way road. On one-way roads, you can go in only one direction and can't return the same way. While she traveled along the pebbled road, a stranger suddenly appeared and asked to take some of the pebbles with her. "Pebbles?" she said to herself, "What is the use?" After a period of consideration, she reluctantly put some in her pockets and went on her way. Having reached her destination, she remembered these pebbles and dipped into her pockets where she put them, to her surprise the pebbles had all turn into valuable diamonds. Two things occurred to that woman. First, she regretted she had not filled all her pockets with pebbles. Second, she was happy that she obeyed the stranger. Life is a one-way journey; you are not coming back again. The pebbles represent all the opportunities you have. You must do all that you can to your brethren. The stranger who urged this individual to collect pebbles represents Pastors, Teachers, Elders, Evangelists, and so forth, encouraging you in the Lord's work. Your final destination is heaven. Some will spend eternity regretting their neglect of good deeds here on earth when every faithful act of services is being rewarded. Take heed and don't miss your opportunities. The word of God is powerful, it is "Truth." It can save lives. It can heal. It can reveal things. It can open your spiritual eyes and bring you closer to Jesus.

Many prophecies have been fulfilled, "That means the bible is truth!" They were written by many prophets and has come to pass in our own eyes. As daughters of Zion we put our complete Trust, Concern, and Faith in God. By my faith, I say to the Lord, "I incubated, nurtured, taught, and led my children to you. By your grace, UPHOLD and SUSTAIN them." By faith we say, "We've trained up our daughters in your ways; as they get older, let them stay close to you." Our faith in God will never be moved. After we have weaned our daughters, we trust God to nestle them in His bosom. After we have hovered over our daughters, we trust God to hide them under the shadow of His wings. There is no doubt we have "FAITH" As women of "FAITH," "We understand the songs of each other's heart." You are daughters of ZION united in love, sisters in "GRACE" looking to Jesus to lead us each day. We are daughters, daughters of Zion.

Signed with Love,

Winnie Smith

Faith Leader

Compiled by Anita Sechesky

Larissa Reed

Chapter 7

Restoration through God's Grace

"How Can You Let Him Get Away with This?"

One day, while doing laundry, that was the question I asked – correction – the question I screamed inside my head...at Him. Yes, Him! The Almighty. The Alpha and Omega. The One I called my God.

Yup. That was me. Laying blame. Deferring responsibility. Back then.

"How can You let him get away with this?"

"Him" was my husband at the time, the father of our two children. In 2005, my son was fifteen months old and my daughter was two and one-half years old.

Getting away with what?

Being a terrifying dad, a frightful husband. Unpredictable, volatile, righteous, angry. Making our home anything but safe, anything but "homey."

There was a time, of course, when all was not like this...or was there?

There was that time I heard a still, soft voice ask me, *"Can you live with this for the rest of your life?"* And I had thought, "No", and was very sure about that for a day...and then married him anyway.

The next seven years of marriage would prove to be the classroom where I would learn – those lessons that one wishes they were born knowing because, boy, those lessons hurt, and hurt they did. But do you know what? It's also where the question "How can You let him get away with this?" would be answered unequivocally.

It was a sunny day two years later. I was alone in the condo. The sun streamed in through the window and hit my skin, warming it. I felt so alive. I could almost feel every pore opening to receive this gift from the sky, this kiss, this affirmation that I was alive and life was good.

How did I get to this place of peace when just two years earlier, life was bleak and dark?

Well, before this place of contentment, things got worse before they got better. They had to. I was living in denial about many things, mostly about the severity of my husband's angry tendencies. As well, my judgment was off about what it was to be a good wife and mother.

You see, I had thought that if I was easy to live with, obedient, agreeable, how could anyone be angry with me? I would be a good wife first. The Good Book said so didn't' it? I was constantly being told, "Wives obey your husbands…" Too bad I didn't' take the time to read the rest of that passage – but that would be part of the life lessons up ahead.

This pattern started young I found out later. This pattern of me doing what I was told.

While taking a course, I remembered how as a child, my mom and dad were arguing, and my mom slammed the milk or cup or something on the table. And in that moment I made the decision to stay quiet, not draw attention, and not to talk back. It was a split-second decision. One I wasn't even aware of making until completing the coursework.

This was supposed to be my recipe for success and yet, even with doing all those things, I had an angry spouse who liked to pull hair, spit mouthwash in my face, and kick my shins.

Part of me felt I deserved it. Part of me rationalized: *Well, no marriage is perfect, everyone has something to deal with. This is just my thing.*

The interesting part is, no one I had dated has these tendencies. Yet I would marry a man who didn't start out violent, but would end up not only hurting me, but my son as well.

Compiled by Anita Sechesky

The day I realized my life was not what I thought it was, and I was not the person I thought I was, I had to walk myself into a police station and surrender to be arrested. The charge: failing to provide the necessities of life.

Three months earlier, my husband was arrested on the same charge, plus assault causing bodily harm. Our son had ended up in hospital after being in the care of my husband. A fall in his crib, or at least that's the story he told the doctors.

After seeing the extent of his injuries, the doctors called the police and Family Services. The injuries did not match the story.

That was when things started to unravel for me. I had a feeling in the pit of my stomach that he was lying, that he could be at fault. That feeling of panic. I wanted to scream, "What did you do?" in front of all the nurses and doctors in Emergency who were running around our son, inserting tubes and taking readings.

Instead, I stayed calm trying to quietly ask him what happened. Not wanting to make a scene. A scene I wished later I had made. He ignored my questions.

As the hours went by, it became obvious that the situation was dire for my son. He had to undergo multiple operations to relieve the swelling in his brain. For one week, my son fought for his life, fought to get out of ICU. And he did. Many miracles transpired in his hospital bed for the three months he was at Sick Kids. Many angels in the form of doctors and nurses brought my son back alive and smiling.

And in that first week of my son being admitted, my daughter was now a ward of the state. After interviewing me, Children's Aid had come to the conclusion that I exhibited all the signs of an abused spouse without me seeing it. It would take getting arrested for me to see it.

I would later tell my cousin, "It was like my brain was in soup, and now my brain is clear."

After all, how could I, a University Graduate working as a teacher for fifteen years, coming from a family of professional parents from a middle-class background, be in this position? HOW THE HELL

DID I GET HERE...in a holding cell...at the bottom of the old City Hall building... waiting for my Bail hearing?

It was really an accumulation over the years of not feeling loved or encouraged, believing the lies I wasn't good enough, it probably was better I had never been born, of agreeing with "I don't' matter" or "I'm not important." So even though I had the outward appearance of being together and confident, inside was a little girl, unsure of her worth, easily convinced of her ineptitude, and ready to please.

Thank God for the counseling and coursework I took over the next two years following my son's admittance into Emergency. Really, I thank God.

Through the work I did, I got to "undo" the negative conditioning my thoughts were telling me. I got to see how, if I had the power to put myself at risk, I also had the power to get out. That one was a huge revelation: I could determine my future, not be a bystander to it.

I saw that who I was did not have to be synonymous with what I had done...THAT had me dancing in the present toward the future and had me soaking up the sun on that sunny afternoon all alone in the condo and feeling so excited about the future.

THAT had me throw off the old disempowering conversations of the past and create newly for the future. I now had the possibility of joy, freedom, and peace, where before I had no possibility. Before I was plodding along, frantically putting out fires, and feverishly looking to prevent others from starting.

I had the opportunity to discover if I wanted to date again or remain a single parent. I had the opportunity to make amends with my daughter – to apologize to her for not keeping her safe and to promise I would keep her safe.

I had the opportunity to see my son walk and talk again after having been told to prepare for the worst during those dark days in ICU.

Since then, I have met a wonderful man. I spoke him into my life six months before meeting him. I said to my God, the very God I had yelled out not even two years before, "Bring a gentle, strong soul who will be my partner in raising these kids, who will be my partner in having a home of peace and ease, who will be my partner in having our dreams come true."

He has been step-dad to these two kids for the past ten years, unwavering in his commitment that we be the best for each other and to each other.

Amazing. Grace. This God of restoration.

Of my soul.

Of my family.

Of my son's physical well-being.

Of my daughter's emotional well-being.

"How could You let him get away with this?"

So that you could learn, dear child

To stand on your own two feet.

That you have everything you need inside of you to make the difference on the outside.

That you would see My power and love.

In the hospital room, in your home, in your heart.

The question has been answered, irrevocably... :)

Larissa Reed was born in Nairobi, Kenya and was forced to leave in 1973. Her father is from Uganda and all South Asians were being expelled by Idi Amin at that time. Arriving in the cold of winter, Toronto, Canada has been home for almost forty-five years. As a child, Larissa loved reading, singing, and playing the piano. She is a graduate of the University of Western Ontario Musical Arts program and Faculty of Education. Larissa has been teaching Vocal Music with the TCDSB for over twenty-five years, and is married with two children. This is Larissa's first writing submission for a publication.

Compiled by Anita Sechesky

Diamond Glitters of Personal Growth

"A woman needs to grow into her own beautiful soul. She must nurture her feminine side with gentle love and wear her unique gifts gloriously with no hesitation to shine brightly for all the world to be blessed by these divine qualities. As she carries out her soul purpose in all the lives that she touches, her spiritual growth and awareness take on a new level of wisdom and enlightenment. Treasure her priceless wisdom and grow from it in your own unique way as well."

~ *Anita Sechesky*

Compiled by Anita Sechesky

Elizabeth Pennington

Diamond Letters

Dear Diamond Sisters;

Today I have you on my mind more than usual.

We have beautiful weather here today. It has been a very rainy season so I'm glad to have the warm sunshine for a change.

Red birds and blue birds are beginning to come back. Spring flowers are blooming and trees are leafing out.

The sun setting is so serine and comforting. A quite peace has fallen over me.

As I am writing this letter to you and watching the sun set, I wonder how you are and what you are doing.

I want to take this time to remind you this is your Life. Live it to the fullest. Never miss a chance to explore new things and meet someone new. Don't look back on life - the past is the past. Always look at completing today and one day at a time for the future. Tomorrow is not a promise.

I may have known you for a lifetime or we may have never met. We may have passed each other at the grocery store or sat across from each other at a restaurant.

It doesn't matter.

You may be young enough to be my daughter or old enough to be my mother or anywhere in between.

It doesn't matter.

It really doesn't matter if we have meet one another or if our paths have simply crossed somewhere sometime.

You may have a different skin color, have a different religious belief, or be from a different culture.

It doesn't matter.

It really doesn't matter what your age is, where you are from, or what culture you come from.

It really doesn't matter what religious beliefs you have chosen. It's your choice and no one else's.

It simply just does not matter.

You are to me my sister!

As I sit here watching the sun set, I hope are you safe from the elements of nature and from any harm of mankind.

I hope you have a warm bed in which to sleep.

I hope you have food to eat and water to drink.

Most of all I hope you have love in your heart.

Those are the things that matter.

However, if you're struggling with life, I want you to know you are respected as an individual and loved as a fellow human being.

If you have "had it all" and now find yourself starting over, know you can accomplish the task of having it all again. This time even better because now you have the experience to help guide you.

If you feel life has let you down take a step back. Look how blessed and rich you are. After all, you're here, aren't you? You have survived all the trials and tribulations that have made you feel let down or caused you pain.

If you feel you are not loved, wrong…you are loved by more people than you think and by people you don't think about. Somewhere, sometime, you have touched a life with your kindness. That person will forever hold a special place of gratitude for you.

We all have times when we feel left out or not worthy to have more. This is a common feeling to have, at least once in our lives. Don't fret over it, instead learn from this time.

If you are being bullied by someone, don't let them take your spirit away from you. Stay in control of yourself. Smile with a soft laughter and walk away. Have empathy for them – they are the one hurting. By being a "bully" or hurting others, they somehow think this makes them "belong" and are in charge, like they are the bigger and most important person in the room. Don't take it to heart that it is about you; it's not.

If you've had a misunderstanding with someone, don't let you pride stand in the way of doing what you know is the right thing to do. Admit it was a misunderstanding and move on. Take time to be an example for the other person. You will never regret it.

If you have married, learn to listen to your partner as much as you expect them to listen to you. If you want love and respect, you must show them you love and respect them. Make decisions together, don't make demands. Above all, learn to forgive. Love is not holding a grudge; it's letting go of the anger.

If you are in a relationship with that "special person," give the relationship your all. Be respectful, be honest, and be understanding. Learn their likes and dislikes. If you feel the love is drifting, take time to talk to them about how you feel. They may be going through something in their world they are not sure how to handle. Let them know you are there for them "if" they want to share with you. This doesn't mean to nag them with why are you doing this or that or the "why haven't you" statements. Don't pressure them. They will share if, and when, it is the right time for them not you.

No matter what has you questioning yourself, take a deep breath and yell out, "I am better than this! I did it once; I can do it again! I will never let anyone or anything ever take my happiness away from me! I will always be my true self!"

As I sit here watching the sun set, I realize I have forgotten to say thank you for being you. Thank you for all you do. Thank you for being here for someone in need. Thank you for giving a smile to a stranger. Thank you for being here for another day regardless of how hard it may be. Someone needs you to be here for them… it could be me!

It's time to go in, so take care of yourself and always remember: you are smart, you are strong, you are beautiful.

You are a very special person.

Love,

Your Sister Elizabeth Ann

Compiled by Anita Sechesky

Michelle LeRoy

Chapter 8

Finding the Harmony within… Once Again

My divorce taught me how to love myself again…After living through the most devastating experience I could ever imagine, as a loving wife and mother, and have it tear me apart actually allowed me to take back control of my own life. I was able put all those broken pieces back together again in the right way… the way that felt the truest to who I was born to be. I no longer had to play a role or live up to anyone's expectations of what a mother, wife, or woman needed to be. My divorce allowed me to re-build myself from scratch.

My divorce affected every aspect of my life and had me re-visit every other relationship I had created including close family and friends, gave me the opportunity to explore how I was showing up in these relationships, and whether or not it was the most authentic and truest version of me as well. I began a journey of re-defining and refining myself and feeling more comfortable than ever in who I am now.

During the lowest point of that journey, there were times I felt like a failure. I felt hopeless, helpless, unlovable, insecure, and even lost. I felt directionless, and that everything we had planned for the future with all the hopes and dreams we had for ourselves and our family fell away.

I realized the devastation was more about the letting go of the marriage but the victory was that I did not need to let go of the love and that was the biggest "A-Ha" moment in that journey. I spent years and years convincing myself I did not love him anymore and after trying so long to accomplish this, I realized that I did not need to do that – it was more harmonious and truer to me to accept, admit that I still loved him, and probably always would regardless of whether or not he felt the same in return. I felt a great peace with this.

During this time, my thoughts were that in order to heal and move forward, I would need to convince myself I did not feel the way I was feeling. But I couldn't; it was not my truth. I had to be in harmony with my heart and it was the only way I would be able to get through this.

Freedom was realizing I could sit in a room and interact with my ex without hating him or feeling angry. Freedom was that I could love him and continue to love him forever and I did not need to change that.

I found my strength in the three pairs of eyes I looked into every day – my children. They depended on me to be the only person who was 100% focused on them and all their needs and dreams and goals. From that day, I would let the sparkle that had seemed to vanish from those innocent eyes be the goal and driving force for EVERYTHING I did.

I focused on speaking with my children, having them talk about the things they loved, what mattered to them, and what they wanted to achieve and accomplish in their lives. I set out to work hand in hand with them to make sure the potential of their dreams was still attainable and seemed possible again.

I realized that my own grief, loss, confusion, sadness, and everything I was still dealing with would have to take a back seat. I was going to have to dig deep to get the strength I knew I was lacking at that moment in order to be the mom I always was and knew I could be once more!

Another aspect of the strength I had was the love from my children. Even through their own pain and suffering, they taught me a level of patience, resiliency, and grace that I am deeply thankful for. Those were the keys that unlocked a lot of my healing through that journey.

I realized that everything I had gone through provided me the ability to be the strong and confident women I am today. I realized that all I have accomplished was due to the fact I needed to rely on me and was able to continually uncover more and more of what I am capable of. My divorce gave me a reason to strive even further than I ever thought possible, having no one to fall back on, and only myself to resort to with three young and impressionable children to set a good example. This propelled me into the successful women, leader, business owner, and entrepreneur I am today.

I appreciated that fact that so many women around me were struggling to truly step into their own full potential and greatness and this journey allowed me to be a beacon of light for them as well!

I also understood that I needed to re-write the definition of mom, wife, friend, and sister for my daughter who looked to me and depended on me to show her the way, as she would be someone's wife one day. I wanted to let her know that she could be anything she wanted to be and that she could get through any situation life would throw her way.

On top of that, it was important for me to demonstrate to my boys the strength of a woman, the importance of believing in themselves, and what they could accomplish in the world. They could be amazing husbands and fathers!

I needed to give back to my children the hope of having a healthy, happy marriage for themselves and what I had learned through my own journey should help them ensure a successful relationship was possible.

The moment I began to take my life back was the most amazing feeling on the planet. When I realized the parts of me I thought were lost, dead, or would never been seen again, were actually still there under a pile of rubble just waiting to be rescued, uncovered, and rediscovered, the only person that could do it was ME!

There was NOTHING and NOBODY that could bring me back to myself but me! There was no one who was going to fill me up and be responsible for my happiness but ME!

It felt great to gain that sense of inner strength and to now know how putting one's happiness into the hands of another would always fall through and fall short. Yes, others can contribute to our happiness, compliment us, support us, and strengthen us, but the fact of the matter is we need to find a way to do all of that for ourselves in order for the brunt of the responsibility to be where it needs to be and that is with each and everyone one of us! No longer will I hand over the role of my happiness to anyone. I am so grateful for this lesson and the enlightenment of re-discovering how powerful, resourceful, and strong I truly am.

Looking back I realize everyone did their best with what they felt could be and would be the right thing to say or the proper advice to give. I thank everyone who did their best to support and help me to move past my love and feelings for him in order to get me back on my feet again. What they did not understand was that I did not want to hear bad things about my ex. I didn't want to be told I needed to stop thinking of him and loving him. I could not stop, I would not stop, and once I gave myself permission to keep loving him, I was able to be set free. I could say with all my heart and in the truest of harmony with myself that I love him, I care about him, and he was and is a great husband, father, and man.

I am also grateful for the ability to know so very deeply that motherhood is the best gift I could have ever received and that focusing on your children during times like this is always the right thing to do. As much as we are feeling pain, their pain is there too. So many children get lost along the way in times like this and I learned that the choice I made to put them first would be a gift to them. It's something they would benefit from forever, and to this day they are reminded of that and appreciate and acknowledge the sacrifices I made now that they are older.

I was able to put all those broken pieces back together again leaving the ones I no longer resonated with in order to shine and bring forth the best of me.

Looking back I would advise anyone else walking through the breakdown of a marriage, or any devastation that shatters a family unit into pieces is to take it one day at a time, continually focusing on the most important things in your life. For me it was the mental, emotional, physical, and spiritual well-being of myself and my children.

I would also suggest to anyone going through a difficult time to avoid remaining bitter, resentful, and/or angry. It's okay to experience these feelings and let them pass, yet holding on to them and keeping them alive within yourself only prevents you from moving forward and being able to bring in positivity and joyfulness once again. You become a magnet from more of what you hold on to, so hold on to the good times, the fun times, what you are grateful for, the lessons you have learned, and let go of the rest. Your future happiness and successfulness depend on it.

I discovered how beautiful I truly am. I understand how powerful I truly am. I also appreciate the level of true joyfulness that I can radiate and choose to express that on any given day at any moment regardless of what I have been through. I felt unstoppable and that I could accomplish anything I put my mind to.

And to anyone reading this, I want you to know that anything you are going through need not define you but only refine you to be the brightest light you possibly can be and that the most beautiful of Diamonds are created under extreme pressure. Through the pain, possibility and potential can be revealed.

Michelle LeRoy is an ACC certified "Kid's Coaching Connection Life Coach" through International Coaching Federation, where she passionately enjoys working with highly sensitive and spiritually aware children. She is also an Energy Medicine Practitioner, Mediation Facilitator, and Holistic Practitioner trained in a vast array of complimentary therapies and modalities. Michelle is highly skilled in many areas of health and wellness. She has also been a valued member of Young Living Essential Oils as an Independent Distributor since 2012. She has successfully achieved the ranking of Gold leadership which puts her into the top 1% for anyone in the company by growing a team of over 2000 members worldwide.

http://michelleleroy888.wix.com/anewearthanewchild

www.thenewearthchildrencentre.com

https://www.facebook.com/groups/newearthchildrensupport/

Compiled by Anita Sechesky

Diamond Glitters of Personal Evolution

"Every woman is gifted with rare and precious qualities created just for her divine journey. It's up to her to discover exactly how intricate and beautiful they are. Not everyone will like you and it's not your fault to own these negative emotions any longer. Instead allow yourself to lovingly release your rejection with love. It doesn't belong to you. The God of our Creation wants you to be free of all that holds you down in this life. Blossom where you are planted in love."

~ Anita Sechesky

Kesha Christie

Diamond Letters

Dear Diamond Sisters;

This life is kind to the overcomer! You are an overcomer! You are stronger than your mind will tell you, with talents that span multiple areas. You possess the ability to bring all of your dreams into fruition. You have greatness in you, all you need to do is believe. Belief can be difficult when challenges attack and cripple your heart. Remember that you are not alone! When it hurts to breathe, keep going. All great things are on the other side of fear, illness, heartbreak, and tragedy. Most people stop in the face of these and fail to live the life they deserve. You are not one of those people. You were made for more!

People talk only of the destination of their dreams and wonder why their hearts are filled with heartache, guilt. and disappointment. Dream Big! The destination is not the reason for their discontentment, they forgot to enjoy the journey. It is the hardest part with its many turns and detours. The journey is necessary! It is in the journey, your strengths shine. Your disabilities disappear and your abilities flourish abundantly. It will take you to and through places never imagined. But there will be setbacks. It is in these low places that the greatest lessons are learned. They equip you for the next level and add clarity to your vision. The journey is a long road, but the rewards are great.

A diamond begins its journey as a lump of coal until pressure is applied – it is the course of nature. Pressure shows up in our lives in many ways, through loss, disrespect, hurt, and shame. Face the pressures; do not become frozen with the weight of these. Refuse to stand still or give up on the journey. Rebel against the fear and pain. Keep moving forward. When the pressure becomes unbearable, reach outside of yourself and help another. Give of your time and your wisdom. You will wear many titles in this lifetime, each with its own set of distractions. Never lose sight of your goals and dreams. There is no greater project that you will ever work on than yourself.

The journey is your teacher; you can stand the pressure without getting burned. Stay focused and embrace love. You must love yourself before you can face this world and its challenges. It is your guide. Take action in love and you will find love wherever you go. Love is found in the places your journey takes you, the people you meet, or in the tribe you build. Everything starts with love! That love is found in you.

Build your strength with each step you take. There will come a time when you will question what you are a fighting for. The road you travel will not always have light nor will you understand its direction. It may be laced with obstacles self-created through doubt while others will be the by-product of the people around you. Their good intentions may not fit your dreams. You can listen and keep your resolve. Each day will be different and some will be a struggle. These are the times your glory shines through. As you continue on, your journey path will take you from the known to the unknown. These changes require focus. Don't get lost in the distraction; stay on target and search for the speck of light on the other side. When the light is difficult to see, create the light within.

Light isn't created from brokenness. You are not broken! You are powerful! You are strong! Where no light is found, you are the light. Hold firm to the decision to live with purpose. Exercise courage, choose faith, and embrace a power greater than yourself. All things are possible – own this belief. Know that you are a conqueror. The victory is yours, but to see it, you must get to the other side. You must keep moving forward.

Gain strength from the words that you speak to yourself and to others. The words you say to yourself can propel you to higher levels or abandon you before you begin. You are enough! You are the only person who can take this journey. There are not destinations in life as you grow; there will be a greater experience opened up to you. No one other than you can live this life better than you. With each lesson, learn to make choices that benefit you. Stay in tune with your needs and desires.

You are not alone! The rewards on this journey ease the burden.

You can be whoever you choose to be. Open your heart and mind to learning each day. It is said that success leaves clues; take control of this life and learn from the best. Stretch outside of your comfort zone! Accept the challenge to learn to be your best. Read, listen, and affirm. The more you flourish, the bigger impact you have on this journey and the greater your achievements.

Surround yourself with supportive people. Let your heart lead you. Explore your talents; let them become your passion. Use your gifts to make a difference. You never know who you are inspiring. Challenge your mind through reading material that excites you and read the things the make you questions where you are in your journey or encourage you to dream bigger. Show vitality is your successes and strength during setbacks. Remember to let go and keep moving forward.

You are resilient! Face your fears, slay your insecurities, and surpass your expectations. Let your courage shine daily in your actions and your attitude. Stand up for yourself, and know you can do anything. It has nothing to do with selfishness, but has everything to do with selflessness.

You cannot give from an empty well. Fill yourself to overflow and give the best that you have to give. Daily remind yourself that you are worthy. Be intentional with this. Speak it, write it, and remember it.

Signed with Love,

Your sister,

Kesha Christie

Motivational Speaker

Compiled by Anita Sechesky

Susan Kern

Chapter 9

What We Put out There Comes Back

In a world of suffering, control, and opposition, we find ourselves constantly bombarded by another tale of challenge and struggle. All we need to do is to turn on the evening news or have a look at the newspaper. It is all around us. If you are like me, you can easily become overwhelmed by the depths to which humanity can sink in its depravity and defilement of fellow humans, animals, and the planet. We hear stories that leave us shaking our heads in disbelief.

Many of us have lived some of these stories first hand. Accounts of sexual assault, domestic violence, discrimination, and hate are plentiful among all walks of life. "Why this is the case?" and "What can be done to change it in the future?" are the questions that sociologists and criminologists explore. They compile data and study the impacts on society. We hear the statistics and they somehow begin to define what is "normal" and therefore, what becomes "okay" in our world experience.

When something becomes normal, it does not make it right. Yet we have all grown accustomed to these stories and experiences as just "the way life is." Inside of us though is a voice that reminds us that it could be different. How we make it different is the opportunity presented to us in our life's journey.

When I was a young woman, and had just finished university, I was looking for employment. I had never really known what I wanted to do, specifically, for a career, but I knew it involved helping to stop the pain and suffering that I saw in the world.

Having grown up in a household where there had been incidents of domestic violence, I knew firsthand how the dynamics unfold. I had no idea how deeply impacted I had been by it, yet I was left with a desire to do something to participate in repairing the damage that victims experienced from such "normal" events.

I ended up working as a Forensic Scientist for the next ten years of my life. That meant I spent my days examining the physical evidence from crimes, doing tests and analysis on that evidence, and submitting reports of my findings to be used in court. On occasion, I had to attend crime scenes and testify in court as an expert witness. I felt a sense of empowerment as a participant in the system that sought to bring justice to these cases even though I wasn't helping to stop the problem.

From the vantage point of the Forensic Scientist, these crimes were our everyday experience. Like other professionals that work in such areas, we experienced tremendous stress. We were often unaware of the stress; it was "normal." Living in this environment, day in and day out, took its toll in my life.

I hadn't realized how burdened my heart had become by dealing with sexual assault, assault, attempted murder, and homicide cases. It was many years after leaving the job that I began to understand that I had been holding a lot of the stress and trauma in my own body. Each case was another layer of stress that was blanketing me. I got sick. I was miserable. I was saddened by the pain that I had dealt with only through objective scientific analysis. In reality, I had become numb to the pain I felt in all areas of my life. There was nothing very shiny about the person I had become because my heart was burdened with the pain of the world around me. How do you shine your own true self out into the world when you have closed yourself off so as to not feel any more? Truthfully, I had become so closed to the world that I had also become closed to myself. Or could it have been the other way around? Was I closed to the world because I had been so disconnected from myself? Something to consider.

I left that world eighteen years ago.

It has been through these past eighteen years that I have begun to explore myself and to find the courage to look inward to that heart that had been so hidden for so long. In the quiet moments between the comings and goings of life as a mother of three, I began to hear the longings in my heart. Hearing and actively listening are not the same things, and it took many years before I could recognize that I was not really living My life. I'm not sure exactly whose life it was, but I certainly wasn't included in it as a priority, nor was I navigating it with my own needs and wants in mind.

The song "This Little Light of Mine" sang out from the television one morning. The kids and I sang along, laughing and smiling. And as we did, it hit me: my true light was not shining. I had dimmed it. So diminished was my light that I was often angry and resentful. The process of coming to terms with the fact that I had allowed that to happen, and even been involved in it directly, was a long journey. It is not easy to look in the mirror and realize that you are the one that got you where you are today. At least, not when you don't like where you are today! Each choice had been a step to where I found myself. The good news? If I had been the one to bring myself there, I could also be the one that could bring me somewhere new!

The first step to reigniting that light for me was to acknowledge and accept what had been, and what was. Tons of self-examination led to tons of self-judgment. It's one thing to review your life; it is quite another to be able to move out of judgment of ourselves, and others. Moving through that phase was the single most powerful part of the journey I have been on. It wasn't easy, but it was simple.

I recognized that I had made choices. The decisions were made from the place I was at in any given moment. I learned to accept that a choice could only reflect what I knew about myself and my situation at the time, and my beliefs about myself and the world. I dissected choices, looking for themes and patterns. Did I choose things that said, "I deserve?" Or did I let others' needs override my own, because I was in a place of "I don't deserve?" Was there a fear that was hidden in my choices? Did I choose to tolerate situations because I didn't feel confident enough to speak up? The answers to these questions were not always comfortable.

As I learned to face the answers and be honest with myself about them, I noticed that what seemed to be unfolding was an interesting trend. I realized that the events in my life had been moving me somewhere. At the time I had not recognized it, but hindsight they say is 20/20. I was seeing that for myself. Over the years I was becoming stronger, clearer, and more aware. I had been growing, even though I didn't see it at the time! I suddenly awakened to the fact that life had not been happening TO me! Each of the challenges or mistakes had served me! They had made me wiser and more confident. The events of my life had really been happening FOR me to come to a place of seeing and honoring my True Self, and giving her a voice.

Reflecting on life events from that perspective made the world of difference. I was able to deeply feel compassion for myself as I realized that there was a scared young girl inside me who was making choices on my behalf based on the fear and doubt she felt. She was me. I was her. I began speaking with this part of me and listening. Life made sense. There was such beauty in the unfolding of my life from this standpoint. All along I was being presented with challenges that were actually opportunities to make new choices based in love instead of fear, and self-worth instead of a lack of worth.

With such a profound new awareness, the Light in me began to shine a bit brighter. Over the years I have learned to tend that inner flame. Stronger, wiser, and more loving is where I now find myself. I no longer perpetuate acts of violence against myself by putting myself down or calling myself an idiot. I wonder if the acts of violence in the world would diminish if collectively we became more tolerant of ourselves and took more responsibility for our feelings. I can only change myself. The more I give my Light permission to shine, the more beautiful my world becomes.

Recently, I was sorting through some old photos and came across a picture of myself from Grade 10. I looked at the girl I had been. I peered deeply into her eyes and remembered some of what she was dealing with in her life and how she was feeling. I saw her, and felt her. I then pulled out photos from various stages through my life, and really started connecting to that person. I ended up with about fifteen images. I could see the journey I had been on reflected in my own eyes! The woman I had become was so much more comfortable in her skin than any of the earlier pictures. I guess that's what it's been about: learning to love myself and allowing that love to spread out into the world.

It seems to me now that the desire I had felt to ease the pain and suffering I saw in the world was a desire to ease my own pain and suffering. Feeling safe to be myself, loving myself, and expressing myself without fear has healed the pain. Maybe that's all any of us really want. And wouldn't that be enough?

Susan Kern, M.Sc. has been on a conscious path of self-exploration and healing for over eighteen years. Having healed a chronic illness in herself, she guides people with challenging life and/or health situations to trust that they have what it takes to heal, grow, and expand into their true self. Susan sees the obstacles in life as opportunities for growth and transformation. A scientist, healer, and teacher, Susan nurtures the vision of people living beyond illusion, where they know they are enough, so they can step into loving, accepting, and trusting themselves as the Divine Humans they truly are.

Anita Sechesky

Chapter 10
Hope Is a Personal Journey Within

To grasp any kind of Hope in one's life, there must be some kind loss, fear, negative influence, impending loss, or insecurity in a person's current state of well-being. This is where having a heart of love and gratitude helps to keep you grounded in your quest for Hope. One must also have that divine connection to source, whatever you perceive it to be. The belief that we are all derived from somewhere outside of who we are in our physical state of being can sometimes leave many unanswered questions in a person's mind. For some people, this means a divine connection to our Creator and God of the Universe – that all knowing, immense presence who sees all and knows all. In these circumstances, there is no question of validity with so many generations aware of this understanding either through faith or ancestral story-telling throughout the years.

Essentially our human spirit searches for a higher influence in which we can transfer our deepest dreams and emotions to a place of ultimate security that is untouchable by all else. It's like we need that soul knowledge and security on some level of spiritual awareness that our divine purpose and destiny is untouchable for those who mean harm in any way possible. I have come into the personal awareness of this very thing through my own observations, whether they were one of the hundreds of previous patients in the nursing homes, hospitals, or general acquaintances I've cared for over the years. It has become obvious to me, based on countless theories and self-help books, that enlightened and heart-centered public figures, motivational speakers, and coaches all discuss how people can be affected by emotional trauma. In doing so, many of them are boldly saying that it's even harmful to personal development and success. What amazes me is despite these resources being so readily available, we often do not give it the acknowledgment and recognition it deserves to be released and healed out of our own lives effectively.

I strongly believe our spiritual physiology is something that we overlook due to the busyness of our lives and therefore it's greatly affected after the most unfortunate of circumstances such as an unexpected health demise or lack of interpersonal strength being developed. If you are constantly working around others who are ungrateful, bitter, and reflecting negative attitude and behaviors, you are going to either absorb some of their rotten energy or you will become just like them. We must strive to understand that no matter what we are going through, our lives are still connected so that what we feel, think, or perceive will be precipitated in our actions and attitudes towards everything that affects us.

We must choose to be open-minded and positively develop into the people we want to become – to understand and appreciate others. As we journey inside our hearts and souls, we will discover a desire pulling us into a mindful state of perpetual gratitude, love, safety, and happiness. We might still find ourselves in moments of unpleasant emotions disrupting our inner calmness and security. It's not an easy journey as many will admit because there will be times of confusion and unbalance in our energy. As confident as we appear, we can still become our worst critic and many times the limitations and perceptions that we hold onto are based upon the most unique, disturbing experiences affecting us during times of weakness and vulnerability.

Living in a world filled with instant gratification as the forefront emotion and strong opposition to a world that you may be choosing which is filled with calmness and placidity, you are going to be dealing with moments of frustration and heavy attitudes that leave you feeling nothing but hopeless and insecure. Does it mean you have lost your sense of confidence in what once was or what will be? I am clearly not one to go that route and based on my own personal experiences I can honestly tell you that if you hold onto your strong spiritual sense and sensibility, you will always find some sort of relief come along side of you and spark that hope once more. You will quickly learn it's not about ego at all. It's about realizing that when no one cares, you have the hope to carry on. When no one calls is the time you will find the answers that were never there. When no one helps is also the moment you can see how clearly you were looking in the wrong direction and your sails are now blowing in a new direction in life. Hope will never let you down if you give it the attention it deserves. Hope is as much philosophical as it is emotional. Hope cannot be fake, just as it cannot be mocked. When you find that you have lost all hope is when you will find it in the most unlikely of places. As individuals of reaction and response, our behaviors are based on the things that we are constantly exposed to. They say habits are easily formed by the unconscious and selective process of who we are choosing to be associated with. Many times, if we don't pay attention to these choices, we mirror the behaviors and actions of these very people. It's not always easy to separate ourselves from individuals we have gotten comfortable being around, regardless of the nature of the connection. Because of this, many will continue to stay in damaging relationships, refusing to step outside of their associations. When this happens, we are left in a stagnated growth, emotionally and mentally, all the while life keeps on going. We continue to age and mature as our appearance changes, but our emotional well-being is slowly damaged. Sadly, we allow so many of our life decisions to fall into a familiar pattern of safety. The potential within us is deeply scarred and languishing because we have not allowed ourselves the proper amount of introspective observation to gain peace and solitude with those painful situations. We become limited in our lives. The Hope that should be there to bring in the successes and well-being is constantly overlooked and cannot blossom into what it can become.

For there to be real hope, happiness, and inner healing, we must often choose the act of forgiveness as the positive channel to release all our negative and pent up energy that will dampen and eventually decay our beautiful spirit. By allowing these new and positive thoughts to heal our damaged emotions, we are shifting the energy around us to that of more peace and gratitude. You see, unforgiveness, anger, hate, and especially hopelessness and all it's negative behaviors are of low vibration and cannot produce anything good as a result. Hope will never come into it's full potential as it was intended to be in our lives, especially if we are still meddling with all those negative and nasty emotions. Too many people are not aware of why they have a false sense of peace and well-being. You see, if one strives for a healthy and confident mindset, all negative attitudes and behaviors must be addressed and determined by what kind of attachments have actually been permitted into one's life. So many times, you will see individuals who attest to having the ultimate achievement we all desire, that of inner harmony and satisfaction, magnified by the power of love, financial security, and social contentment. They want you to believe they've arrived. It's up to you to determine what you see and what they want you to see. Every single person must interact and grow from their interpersonal relationships and daily connections with others. There's just no way you can avoid this human experience, unless you completely shut yourself off from interactions and FaceTime with family, friends, neighbours, co-workers, or colleagues. As we become more connected with those outside our inner circle, we then start to examine ourselves differently, as every connection brings its own set of experiences. For example, more setbacks, failures, challenges, disappointments, and opportunities to grow and develop into our best self yet, all of which are prime opportunities to be let down, lose hope, and shift our perspectives easily to that of isolation and pain.

Whatever the event, life will always present us many chances to change our responses; it does not always have to end that way. Our outcomes are solely determined by our reactions, and attitudes play a huge part of our international temperature gauge. Are we warming up to someone or did we choose to hold something over them? Are we allowing things to slide or are still in a rift with something that happened months or years ago? The choice to be at peace and hold onto hope despite everything is always ours to make.

When we come to understand that being centered is when the heart is at peace, our divine connection to God of our universe becomes a confidence that is unwavering and reassures us in times of uncertainty that we can get through just about anything if we believe in ourselves and something bigger than we can conceive. These emotions are so connected and correlate on so many levels, that's why we must come to the full awareness that everything is a choice and our emotional state is also a choice in which we get to choose how we will perceive everything that comes in to our fate. We don't get to walk away, ignore, and then complain when everything goes wrong. It's our fault when we fail at getting the expectation of joy or even hope, because once we understand that Hope is a personal choice, we have taken all the power away form those who would want us to believe otherwise, such as those bullies in our classrooms, neighborhoods, or places of employment. Yes, you can even be the owner and boss of your company and have bullies trying intimidate you and change the temperature of your environment as they feel they can get away with pressure tricks and tactics that make you feel like you are losing your mind and cannot manage your business. I am here to tell you that once you stay grounded and get back on track with your goals and ambitions, you'll find your inspiration will start coming from out of nowhere. People who are in alignment with your beautiful vision will be drawn to you. The energy will shift and those who have no interest will move on. You learned a lesson not to give up on the hope that you created for yourself. Your vision is giving others hope, who have none. Your unique artwork is inspiring others. Your creative music is lifting up so many souls. Your cooking is creating appetites for the most discerning of palates. Don't give up! Don't give in! You've got this! For someone to achieve this state of personal success without the applaud and validation from others, it is choosing to be in simple gratitude and appreciation of oneself. You must understand that life is a story you get to co-create with the people in your life as much as with the universe. Our emotional state is created by our reality, based on our attachment to the outcome, so when seeking an experience in life, we must comprehend that there is a requirement of us to also put effort, and as much hope as possible, into developing the miracle of peace, through mediation, forgiveness, prayer, or acceptance of a situation. We may find ourselves in situations where we cannot get into a meditative or calming state because there's so much happening around us, and we can't achieve the balance and stability we need. It's at these moments that a trained mind will follow the rules of grounding oneself into a place of security. We can do this through visualization, prayer, or positive affirmations. Most people choose to associate miracles and positive outcomes to the understanding that they have deposited a portion of faith, moral thoughts, and optimistic attitudes towards their anticipated outcome. Often, life's painful experiences are the contributing factors causing people to demand within themselves that which makes them invincible. This is also an intricate factor why many people lose hope so quickly without realizing it themselves.

Throughout life's journey, the human spirit perseveres through many difficulties that would have otherwise taken us down had we not had an ounce of peace that prevails. Developing and seeking a life of unconditional hope commences in early childhood and is most often influenced by the content we are exposed to from other human behaviors regardless of who they are and where they fit into our lives. It will impact the very essence of that person who experiences these situations to determine what level of hope they have in their lives and do they want to maintain it regardless of whatever it takes. These experiences may include the loss of a loved one, life-threatening conditions, a devastating diagnosis, traumatic and abusive relationships, family rifts, as well as other moments not fondly recalled. As we choose to remember, what happens may not be directly associated to who you are, but life will always give you experiences aligned to the vibrational energy of those you are closely connected with. You might even be a receiver of the energies from those you are not even associated with any longer. The very nature that you have interacted with someone at any given point, vibrationally sets you up for some kind of universal reminder of that person. That's why we must conscientiously strive to develop an intrinsic attitude of unlimited and unconditional hope that permeates from within. We are all responsible beings and emotional intelligence is the reason we have the capacity to gain this ownership of our lives despite our daily challenges.

By recognizing that your life has equal value, just as those you are associated with, allows your higher self to rise and join with others on a more dependable and genuine level. This is a huge deal for those who have suffered from abandonment or offensive and disturbing experiences where they were susceptible enough to allow circumstances to traumatize them so. Although this may have happened unexpectedly, it *does* not mean it was the victim's fault in any way, shape, or form. It just means that the awareness of the pain has reinforced the individual enough to move them from a victim mind-set to self-empowerment and strength to maintain a level of hope and healing involving forgiveness, not only of the individual who inflicted the wrong, but an acceptance to forgive one's self for being in the situation to begin with.

People will carry on doing the same things repetitively, assuming a different result each time, and still not finding the hope and inspiration they are seeking after. Unfortunately, they don't recognize that the resolution is acquainting themselves to a whole new viewpoint that unlocks windows of opportunities, allowing them the ability to heal, evolve, and fluently grow with new and healthier perspectives. I often wonder about those who feel utterly hopeless and how it would impact the lives of those who feel trapped and isolated. Nothing is hopeless if they would only choose to have an abundance mindset and learn to appreciate and love the life they have been blessed with. They must develop a constant method of compassion and love, allowing the peace to be recognized in their connections with others. Letting go of sadness consequential to unforgiveness and pain will permit the stagnant, adverse, and damaging energy and low vibrations to be released from their energetic composition. As they choose to make an effort in their thought processes, emotional intelligence, verbal and emotional triggers, as well as the behavioral feedbacks around them remain positive with higher positive energy from the power of love that envelopes the peaceful aura around and through, creating a simple but significant change in thoughts, actions, and external attitudes. Once we choose to continue attracting more positive and peaceful experiences, it will begin healing our very souls.

Examining my own life, I have also experienced the struggle to hold my peace when I had no control over the outcome based on actions of the other individual involved. I learned that if there are unsettled events in my life, there will always be some sort of direct disruption and blockage of peaceful blessings and gratitude. This is what permits a renewal of perspectives to create a life shift in future viewpoints and its results.

Hope is personal journey, but it is conditional on the relations of the people you are associated with. However, it is one of the most powerful things you can do by choosing to step into. May your journey be filled with unlimited hope.

Anita Sechesky is the Founder and CEO of Anita Sechesky - Living Without Limitations Inc. She is an RN, CPC, Best-Seller Publisher, Multiple International Best-Selling Author, as well as a Law of Attraction and NLPP.

Anita is also the CEO, Founder, Owner, and Publisher of her company LWL PUBLISHING HOUSE.

Currently she has successfully branded 300 International Best-Selling authors in the last three years. LWL PUBLISHING HOUSE is a division of her company, in which she offers coaching, mentoring, motivation, marketing, and of course publishing services for her clients. 2016 marks the addition of two new branches in LWL PUBLISHING HOUSE dedicated specifically to children's books of inspiration and learning, and also fiction and non-fictional single author books.

Working with Anita at one of her "LWL INSPIRED TO WRITE" workshops, Webinars or one-to-one support, will equip you to step out of your comfort zone fearlessly! Anita's solo book entitled "Absolutely You - Overcome False Limitations & Reach Your Full Potential" was written in less than four weeks and she can teach you how to do the same!

CEO of Anita Sechesky – Living Without Limitations Inc., Founder and Publisher of LWL PUBLISHING HOUSE.

Best-Seller Mentor, Book Writing Coach, Registered Nurse, Certified Professional Coach, Master NLPP and LOA Practitioner, multiple International Best-Selling Author, Workshop Facilitator & Trainer, Conference Host, Keynote Speaker.

Join my Private Facebook group: LIVING WITHOUT LIMITATIONS LIFESTYLE.

With over 960 members, we offer exclusive prizes, co-authoring opportunities, Random Contests with FREE Publishing possibilities, "Inspired to Write" Webinar classes, and more - http://bit.ly/1TlsTSm

Please visit our Facebook page: LWL PUBLISHING HOUSE

Website: www.lwlpublishinghouse.com

Email: lwlclienthelp@gmail.com.

Join my Private Facebook group:

LIVING WITHOUT LIMITATIONS LIFESTYLE: Exclusive prizes, co-authoring opportunities and Random Contests with FREE Publishing opportunities. http://bit.ly/1TlsTSm

Compiled by Anita Sechesky

Elaine Cray

Chapter 11

How to Be a Friend in the Worst of Times

The depth and strength of a friendship is often measured in times of need. In our darkest hours, our most turbulent times, is when we require the most support. This is when we sometimes discover how truly important a friend is. These times can test the authenticity of a friend.

Many years ago, a friend of mine went through one of the most heartbreaking times in her life.

She lost a child. Her baby was still born.

The pain was deep and paralyzing. She withdrew into a very dark place and eventually became numb. The sadness and despair was horrific and agonizing to watch.

Her and I were a part of a group of girls that hung out together. We met in high school. Our friendships centred around having a good time: shopping, gossiping, going dancing, and tanning at the beach. We slept at each others' houses and stayed up all night sharing secrets, or consoled each other when there was a heart break. We supported each other, motivated each other, and sympathized for one another when one of us was grounded or failed a class. Eventually graduating and finding jobs, we were ready to take on the world. Through the years, we all had ups and downs, bumps in the road. Tears were shed and shoulders were offered. But none of us had faced real tragedy. So, when my friend lost her baby, we were suddenly confronted with the true test of our friendships.

Many of her friends disappeared – moved on with their own lives. Some sent flowers and cards. The very closest of us reached out by calling. She didn't answer.

Eventually she answered the phone. Through heart-wrenching sobs, some of the details of what she had endured started emerging. I remember holding the phone, my hand shaking and shedding my own tears. I listened to her weeping through the phone, wishing I could be with her and hug her. I didn't say much, hesitating to say anything at all. Not knowing what to say. I certainly didn't want to upset her more but I also didn't want her to think I didn't care. I mustered up the courage to ask very painful, awkward questions. All of which she answered. In fact, it seemed that she had been wanting to talk about it. That she needed to talk about it.

I decided it was time for a visit, but I didn't bring flowers or a card. What was the point? It wouldn't make her feel any better. I did bring her a home-made casserole and some baking that she could freeze. I figured she wouldn't be eating properly and certainly wouldn't be up to cooking.

We sat side by side. I hugged her. There were long stretches of silence and lots of crying. There was nothing comfortable about the visit. This is when I learned that in order to support someone, we have to be willing to step out of our comfort zone. My being there was important.

In the following days I would leave messages, "Just calling to say I love you." Other times, when she didn't want company, I would leave things on her doorstep wanting her to know I was thinking of her.

Many weeks, maybe it was even months, later I called to see if I could pop by. Promising not to stay long if she wasn't up to it, she reluctantly agreed. I showed up with coffee and treats and immediately tried to engage her in some small talk. She seemed annoyed with me and impatient. The frustration was written all over her face and I could cut the air with a knife! I asked her if there was anything I could do for her, and even suggested we go to a movie. That's when she exploded. "What are you here for? What do you think you can possibly do to make me feel better? Can you put my son in my arms? Can you turn back the clock?" She yelled, she swore, she called me names. She threw her empty coffee cup across the room. I jumped to my feet. "That's right. Go one. Leave.

Get out. Go away like everyone else." But I didn't leave. I started screaming, swearing, and punching the couch because I was angry too. I was pissed off! One of my best friends lost her child. And I felt like I was losing my friend. I was mad that everyone else seemed to abandon her and move on as if nothing was wrong. I picked up my own cup in a fit of rage and tossed it across the room, only mine wasn't empty and coffee splattered everywhere, including all over my raging friends face. We both stopped. I gasped. Jane stood frozen, mouth agape. We stared at each other for a moment. Her with coffee dripping from her nose, me with mucus and tears dripping from mine. We simultaneously broke out in hysterical laughter. Crazy side stitching cackles. We must have lost our minds! We managed to pull ourselves together. Joined by our grief, we clung together in a desperate embrace. "Thank you" she whispered. "I love you" I whispered back. It was cleansing and cathartic. The beginning of a journey to healing.

The next time we got together, I arrived with a picnic basket filled with goodies, bread, cheese, fruit, and chocolate, but most importantly…lemon vodka. I told her to grab her sweater 'cause we were going out. She objected, and I knew she would. I insisted, and I think she knew I would. It was with great trepidation that she stepped outside and shut the door behind her. It must have taken every ounce of courage to face the world. I put my arm around her shoulders squeezing her tightly to my side. "I'm so proud of you Jane. I know this isn't easy."

We spent the afternoon sitting under a tree in a field, eating, talking, and wiping tears. We pondered the meaning of life and death; questioned our faith and purpose. "Cheers," lifting a glass in the air and holding one out for Jane, I made a toast. "Here's to Matthew. He may not be in our arms, but he will always be in our hearts." We shot back the vodka and gagged. Jane leaned over and grabbed the bottle to pour two more. With a raised glass, "To Matthew" she sighed.

She was vulnerable and raw. I was protective and nervous. There was a breakthrough that afternoon, a glimmer of light appeared in her eyes. Hope. I had faith that she was going to be okay.

Months passed and soon it was years. Time eased some of the pain.

Like an open wound begins to close or a broken bone fuses back together, the scars are always there as reminders, but life goes on.

I endured some turmoil of my own years later and She was there. She was my rock, my sponge, my sounding board, and my ammunition.

When we reminisce on times past, our young and foolish days, mistakes we made, fun we had and pain we endured, we always talk about how strong and powerful our friendship was, IS. We agree, we have embodied the definition of what a good friend is and what it means to be a friend in the most difficult of times.

Knowing that we can trust each other to always be honest. Sometimes brutally, usually gently. We don't always have to be at our best and when we are not, the other will always be accepting, patient, and supportive. Friendship isn't always about what you get from the other person, sometimes it's about what you can give. Sometimes no words can speak louder than a hundred, that no time or space or distance can lessen the quality of a friendship. Both of us are committed to empowering the other. There is no room for jealousy.

We have discovered that to be a friend in the worst of times, it may require one of us to sacrifice. It might mean sparing a moment on a day when you barely have time to breath. It might mean stepping outside of your comfort zone.

Being a genuine friend means allowing the other to be true to themselves and understanding and respecting that we won't always agree and that's okay.

It's in knowing that everything you do, as a friend, comes from love and a mutual affection.

Compiled by Anita Sechesky

Elaine Cray is a loving wife, a mother of three girls, an animal rights champion, and a Professional child care provider for twenty years. Her second child was born with a rare genetic syndrome that resulted in a developmental disability. Elaine saw a need to help the Special Needs community foster friendships, so she developed a grass roots initiative: The Special Friends Network. Elaine has been writing poetry and short stories since childhood. Recently those writings have remained a very personal and private pastime. Through her experience as a Best-Selling author and contributor in #Hope and now in Shine like a Diamond, Elaine strives to touch and inspire others.

crayzedx5@hotmail.com

www.thespecialfriendsnetwork.ca

Compiled by Anita Sechesky

Diamond Glitters of Courage

"A woman's heart beats for many in her life, but her love is fierce as it is gentle to protect those within her immediate care. Nurture your true self with gratitude, grace, and acceptance that not everyone will receive your love and spirit as theirs to treasure. This is where your inner strength flourishes with unselfish love for self-perseveration in times of adversity, rejection, pain, and fear."

~ *Anita Sechesky*

Kesha Christie

Diamond Letters

Dear Diamond Sisters;

"I AM ENOUGH." Knowing your value is the most important lesson in life. Some are born with this knowledge and it never leaves them. Others lose themselves little by little in the daily tasks of life. They set aside uniqueness to embrace comfort, attempting to please others and causing harm to themselves like anxiety, weight gain/loss and stress. If you are in the latter category, you are not alone. Life changes moment to moment, shifting from struggles to triumphs and back again. But losing sight of our value makes it difficult to adjust to these shifts.

We can take control. Begin by accepting yourself and knowing that you are enough. Acknowledging this gives us the strength to nurture our gifts. It allows us make choices from a place of confidence and power. Take on the force of life by embracing the mantra "I AM ENOUGH" and eliminate fear. Stand firm in self-assurance that you are enough; stop looking to others for acceptance. Instead, let others make the choice to accept you as you are and not for whom they want you to be. Open the door to those who want to be a part of your circle/tribe and close the door to others who make you feel small. Let those people fall away. Surround yourself with a like-minded community and focus on positive thoughts. Change is constant. You will survive. As we stand in unison, remember that above it all "I AM ENOUGH." All the time.

Kesha Christie

Motivational Speaker

Anita Sechesky is the Founder and CEO of Anita Sechesky - Living Without Limitations Inc. She is an RN, CPC, Best-Seller Publisher, Multiple International Best-Selling Author, as well as a Law of Attraction and NLPP.

Anita is also the CEO, Founder, Owner, and Publisher of her company LWL PUBLISHING HOUSE.

Currently she has successfully branded 300 International Best-Selling authors in the last three years. LWL PUBLISHING HOUSE is a division of her company, in which she offers coaching, mentoring, motivation, marketing, and of course publishing services for her clients. 2016 marks the addition of two new branches in LWL PUBLISHING HOUSE dedicated specifically to children's books of inspiration and learning, and also fiction and non-fictional single author books.

Working with Anita at one of her "LWL INSPIRED TO WRITE" workshops, Webinars or one-to-one support, will equip you to step out of your comfort zone fearlessly! Anita's solo book entitled "Absolutely You - Overcome False Limitations & Reach Your Full Potential" was written in less than four weeks and she can teach you how to do the same!

CEO of Anita Sechesky – Living Without Limitations Inc., Founder and Publisher of LWL PUBLISHING HOUSE.

Best-Seller Mentor, Book Writing Coach, Registered Nurse, Certified Professional Coach, Master NLPP and LOA Practitioner, multiple International Best-Selling Author, Workshop Facilitator & Trainer, Conference Host, Keynote Speaker.

Join my Private Facebook group: LIVING WITHOUT LIMITATIONS LIFESTYLE.

With over 960 members, we offer exclusive prizes, co-authoring opportunities, Random Contests with FREE Publishing possibilities, "Inspired to Write" Webinar classes, and more - http://bit.ly/1TlsTSm

Please visit our Facebook page: LWL PUBLISHING HOUSE

Website: www.lwlpublishinghouse.com

Email: lwlclienthelp@gmail.com.

Join my Private Facebook group:

LIVING WITHOUT LIMITATIONS LIFESTYLE: Exclusive prizes, co-authoring opportunities and Random Contests with FREE Publishing opportunities. http://bit.ly/1TlsTSm

Leah Lucas

Chapter 12

Compiled by Anita Sechesky

That Negative Energy is Unhealthy

I'd like to start off this chapter with some phrases that I think everyone in the world has heard at least one time in their lives:

"What comes around goes around"

"Karma"

"You reap what you sow"

"Negativity breeds negativity"

Any of those sound familiar to you at all? Everyone would agree those expressions are very well known. I had ALL of those said to me almost daily for a number of years. Obviously when people are telling you to adjust your attitude in some way, it's likely to set off one of two emotions in your mind: either negative or positive. Question is, which one will you chose and do you know how to even make that choice? Positive is healthy. Negative is not healthy.

Here is my experience with negative energy and how it has played out in my life in the last eight years.

I was in a wonderful place in my life in 1989. I was with the man I planned to marry, had moved to Seattle, and started a great career in banking. I got married, earned a job promotion, started a family, and then bought a house. I had two kids and great life at that point. I was so lucky and grateful that my spouse at the time had an amazing job which allowed me to stay home with our kids after they were born. I was a very positive woman, loved my life, had many friends and a happy family. However, during my second pregnancy in 2003, my positives in life began slipping into darkness so much, that the negatives would later consume me to a point that all I knew was anger, rage, blame, and sadness on all levels. I got sick during my pregnancy with my son. I ended up with a condition called interstitial cystitis that I would then battle for almost seven years after his birth. This event lead me into the deepest darkest days of my life. I lived in hell for many long and lonely years. I got lost from within. I lost myself, my thoughts, my being, and then lost all control of emotions and judgments. Then I spiraled into the world of alcohol and drugs. I lost my entire happiness to those things during that time. I never even realized the phrase that stuck with me the most (negativity breeds negativity) was the one I was sending out into the universe. It was coming around full circle and I was so unhappy all the time. Negativity breeds just that. Negativity. Unhealthy is all unhealthy energy. I had not yet discovered the true power of positivity until a couple years later.

I had been spending night after night reading on social media sites all kinds of quotes and phrases that I felt applied to my state of mind at the time. I was ready and willing to point my anger, rage, and really all the issues that were in my mind, into the phrases I was reading, then posting hundreds of negative posts on my page. Without even knowing, it was creating a circle of negatives that were only coming back tri-fold and causing me more difficult situations. I had spent hours daily blaming everyone else EXCEPT myself for all that was wrong with my life. The stress of voicing all that. The tears, heartache, sadness, then darkness added fuel to the fire causing so much emotional trauma on every level of my being, I was physically sick. I had no clue that by only sending out negative energy, I was manifesting more of the same into my life. During this time, many things happened to me that I now, on some level, feel as if I brought upon myself. I had survived being raped, and I would later lose my home to fire, forcing me to become homeless for a summer. When I thought that was the worst thing that could ever happen to me, eight months later I would lose my mother to lung cancer.

However, during all my negative postings and blaming everyone else, someone was reading all of it. She is a dear friend who was reading all my pain through social media. One day she messaged me and asked one question. "Can I flip the negatives around and only think and post positives thoughts for thirty days?" I thought, "Hmmm. I guess I can try that." And I did. That's when I saw and felt a huge mind and energy shift from deep within myself – deep from inside my soul. I spent every day reading, posting, and thinking only positives thoughts. I saw a phrase that I loved and held onto it. My very favorite, to this day, is "Live, Laugh, Love." It's now my motto in life and how I live along with a code of five words. Those are: Trust, Love, Loyalty, Honesty, and Faith.

After the thirty days of only posting and reading positive phrases, things in my life started to change. Although I was obviously still going to feel the after effects of speaking all that negativity into the universe (hence the phrase "What comes around, goes around") Karma, I think, fit well for what happened with losing all my family, all my friends, then my house, plus my business, and everything material in my world except my actual real life. I suffered so much heavy losses in such a very short time that I felt sick in my body most of the time. During the truly rough times though I was living a fight or flight response life daily. I was just trying to survive, but still only sending out positive vibes into the universe. I learned in one summer the true meaning of Law of Attraction. I was homeless at the time after the fire, my mother was terminally ill from lung cancer, and I dropped everything in my world to go and be with family during her last year of life with us. I know that during these days, in my pure state of only survival mode, I did not allow myself to actually get sick. If I did, my mind was too crazy busy with everything else that I didn't notice just how much the past events were creating so much compounded stress on my entire body, both inside and out.

After the loss of my mother, and upon returning home to Seattle, Washington, things were slowly getting better day by day for me. I sat by my mother's side only thinking positives for my life and creating a baby-step plan to building my life back to some sort of normal again. While I was with her though, I managed to process and forgive, then let go of most of my past experiences, emotionally and spiritually. I learned the hardest lesson in life I think one can master: forgiving myself, then everyone and everything that had caused me emotional pain. I let my entire past go. Forgave it all. Then I moved forward having only total faith in God.

Upon returning to Seattle, I got a job quickly, and positive vibes kept going. They kept coming right back for me! Those positives led to a better job, then better housing. I felt good mentally, but physically I was starting to suffer. I had not allowed myself to notice ever being sick because I was on a mission to return home to my kids. Once I made it back, the physical issues began. It started out as catching colds often to having headaches, and not being able to sleep well at all. That led to infections requiring medications, which I just recently learned was compounding a serious stomach issue that I had no idea was plaguing my body. I suffered seizures trying different medicines to help me cope with the major trauma and PTSD emotions. I started grinding my teeth which resulted in them cracking. That meant more doctor and dentist visits, and more meds.

Finally, after moving and being allowed the time and space I needed to grieve and process my mother's death, I began to suffer major health issues. Just recently (this is now where I bring the negative energy is unhealthy verses positive energy creating health from within into my story) I was out celebrating my boyfriend's birthday with friends when suddenly I felt very sick to my stomach, so we left early for home (I knew I had stomach issues for months; just never knew the cause). A few hours later I was being taken by medics to the hospital with internal bleeding of unknown causes. In the ER, tests confirmed that my internal bleed was so extensive that I would need not just one blood transfusion, but two! I was so scared and had no idea what was even happening. Nothing could have prepared me for this life-changing event. After hours of tests, meds, and scans, it was confirmed that I had suffered major internal bleeding caused by Peptic Ulcers which were directly caused by compounded stress and medications.

This illness was now the third time I had come very close to death in my lifetime. I spent two months in bed recovering from the bleeding. The lesson here, at least for me, is that I need to keep my thoughts positives in order to stay alive and healthy. Positives thoughts are the key to everything. Negative thoughts are the demise of all things healthy and happy in my life.

I urge you to flip your thoughts around. Make the change to positive thoughts and see what you can manifest into your own lives. I promise you good things will start happening for you and life will eventually get better. It's basic Law of Attraction, and just takes time and conscious efforts to keep the positive flow going. Then it returns full circle.

Here's a tip to keep in the back of your mind when trying to stay positive in unsettling and negative times and situations flows: Energy where your attention goes.

Remember that you are the creator of your own destiny. So I invite you to shine like the diamond in the rough that you are.

Leah Lucas

Leah Lucas is a single mother of two amazing teens. She is starting her Life Coaching Certificate and spends most of her time learning on her own doing research. Leah has fought hard to earn her place in life after surviving the lose of her home to fire. Her smile and outgoing personality make her a joy to be around. She has an amazing positive light surrounding her. Leah spreads love and wisdom through her life experiences, enjoys family time, and scrapbooking her memories.

Lucas_Leah@hotmail.com

Compiled by Anita Sechesky

Diamond Glitters of Unlimited Love

"A woman's mind is multi-faceted with the concerns of all she cares for. This is her secret super-power that enables her mind to focus on things of great importance in her world. Encourage her to never stop being who she is. This is what our world needs more of: unselfish love to bring hope for so many generations yet to come. Let's begin right now with ours."

~ Anita Sechesky

Melisa Archer

Diamond Letters

Dear Diamond Sisters;

Ever since I was a little girl, my mom has been my biggest cheerleader. Mom would tell me I could do anything. Mom would constantly give me positive reinforcement. This helped me to have the confidence to do what I want, to try anything and everything...and I did.

I want to share with you her excitement that has guided and helped me through life's many trials and tribulations. She cheered me on to become the best version of myself. Sometimes you just need someone to listen as you vent, just agree with you, or simply just acknowledge how you feel about life.

You deserve to experience my mom's pep talk:

> "You can do it!
>
> Reach for the stars!
>
> I'm so proud of you!
>
> You go for it!
>
> YOU are the BEST!
>
> You make my heart sing.
>
> I love you so much!
>
> You make me proud!
>
> I'm behind you 100%.
>
> Never let anyone put you down.
>
> Try your best.
>
> You will do well.

> I am here for you.
>
> You are my biggest accomplishment.
>
> Spread your wings and fly.
>
> Feel my hug.
>
> I love you, always."

Of course ninety percent of what you say is actually through your actions. With Mom, it was always her eye contact while speaking to me, and her commitment to driving me to my endless list of activities. When someone is putting his or her own dreams aside to make yours happen, it inspires you to really shine. Yes, at times it felt for me that my dreams were her dreams, and my accomplishments were really our accomplishments. As an adult, I have come to realize that once you have a child, you are no longer the star. You have passed the torch to become a cheerleader wanting the best for your child. For extra encouragement, envision your mom, a lovely lady, or supportive man speaking from the list above to you.

Of course I am an "A" personality, so if I did not want to do something there was no coaxing me. However, if I want something, I will work, study, and practice so hard that I am over prepared. This is vital for anyone who wants to achieve. It takes 6,000 – 10,000 hours experience to become a professional in a field. It comes down to dedication. Are you willing to put in the time and effort to achieve your dream or goal? Keep in mind everyone has the same twenty-four hours in a day. Those getting ahead are often utilizing their hours differently, efficiently.

Here is a big secret: Just start. I have had an advantage over others because of my willingness just to start. It is expected that you won't be perfect on your first attempts. You can only learn to do things a better way, once you have tried some wrong ways. There is a saying that my dad would always say to me: "Try to learn from my mistakes. Life is too short for you to have to make them all yourself."

Another big lesson to pass on: Luck is preparation meeting opportunity. If you have a goal in mind and focus on preparation then you will be ready if an opportunity should present itself. No one else can force you to have the dedication of preparation. This needs to come from your fire within.

How do you start the fire from within? What do you want? What do you desire to do or be? This is where you need to draw your strength.

To add fire to your flame, small victories are a must. It is very unrealistic to think that you will hit a home run the very first time that you swing a bat. If you first learn how to hold and swing the bat with proper body mechanics from top to bottom will help in balance. If you learn to keep your eye on the ball and feel the contact of ball to the bat you are on the right track.

First, focus on the steps that you need to learn to hit the ball. Next, learn how hard you must hit the ball to have it count as a home run. These steps are getting you closer to the prize. Is there more to learn? Yes, the timing. The time it takes to get your bat from your shoulder to meet the ball in front of the plate. This requires you to be patient and remain focused in preparation. Learning the angles you can use the bat to send the ball in different areas of the field is also good technique. From this example, you can see that hitting the homerun has less to do about just hitting the ball but more about the conditioning that is needed, so that your body will react from muscle memory with proper training. Remember, goals are to be Specific, Measurable, Attainable, Realistic, and set to a Timetable. Be SMART!

Self-confidence. This is all on you. Repeat the list in a mirror. Once you have the feeling and know that you can reach your target for the day, get your energy going towards your goal. If you want to hit that homerun, then you need to get started with hitting some balls.

There will be signs that you are going to make your goal. If not, you should alter your current track. This is important. If your goal is not realistic or attainable, it is best to reevaluate. Do some soul searching and decide what you want to spend your life-minutes doing.

Recharge your soul as needed. Time and energy is not wasted when you invest in bettering yourself for others through service. If you spend a percentage of your time grounding yourself with helping animals, those in need, or volunteering, I have found that you receive more guidance. The secret to shining is helping others to shine in their own unique way.

I encourage everyone to cheer others on so there are more shining stars in this world.

Michelle Francis-Smith

Compiled by Anita Sechesky

Chapter 13

Multi-Faceted Woman - How to Manage Life

In the beginning, at the moment of that first breath, there was YOU! A being who was blessed to make the passage into this world and now the rest after God is up to you...

My sole purpose is to create soul connections. I've been blessed to have found many outlets for this in my life. I truly believe that one of God's greatest purposes for me is to be a lover of the unloved and a healer for the wounded and often unseen. I always try to remember this great responsibility in each moment of my life. Fulfilling this mission is my greatest motivation for all that I am and all that I do.

I have soul-searched most of my life, now thirty-nine years of age, wanting to realize my purpose and uncover my spiritual gifts. With each challenge, triumph, and complete breakdown, I have been propelled into deeper levels of understanding and the more I learn, the more curious I am. This will likely never change because my thirst for knowledge is endless and I believe we learn more about ourselves through our experiences. As I share some of my experiences and the lessons I have learned through them, I am driven to share freely in hopes to motivate others as they are inspired and grow. This is a philosophy I have taken into all the classrooms, conference rooms, small group facilitations, treatment rooms, even casual conversations on the neighborhood park bench. My thirst to understand what my life is, all it is meant to be used for, and to prompt others to see their intrinsic value excites me and helps me see the endless possibilities for all of our lives.

"Who are you Superwoman? How do you make all of this work, doing all that you do and having so many roles you play in your life?"

I can't even count the amount of times comments like those have been directed my way. I struggle sometimes with mixed reactions to this because I think anyone out there striving to create reality out of their dreams is pretty powerful with super person qualities! When I reflect on these questions with some of the incredible women in my life, we almost always conclude with the same thing: it's damn hard and at times feels almost impossible to DO IT ALL! From running multiple businesses, managing households, being active in your children's lives, maintaining relationships, and trying to remain present in all that you do, the challenges are great, and the rewards often difficult to measure by any average standards. That all being said, do I believe I can DO IT ALL? Well surprisingly YES!

My appetite for life is limitless and it follows me both personally and professionally, as I dream bigger, wider, and higher. I have come to this conclusion: I can DO IT ALL, just not ALL at the same time and definitely NOT ever successfully alone.

While on a bumpy ride to the emergency room on a Thursday evening, after collapsing suddenly at one of my multiple job sites, I became gravely aware that my quest to Do IT ALL was coming at a price I could no longer afford to pay. After two decades of moving too quickly through my life, trying to be the best helper, mother, lover, friend, teacher, therapist, and the list continues, I was faced with my limitations and it scared me into reactions and later careful actions. So used to being in the one up position as the provider, nurturer, and caregiver, I had lost site of the fact that I am all the people I touch, teach, and support. When did I exactly lose sight of this? Or had I just not ever really considered this as possible? On this particular day the Paramedic who rode to the hospital in the back with me did more than stabilize my vitals, her questions about what my typical day looked like and her challenging words on why I was doing as much as I was, helped to save my life. Lying in the hospital that evening for hours undergoing multiple tests, I made it my mission to restructure my life. The following day began my new approach to living including all that I loved but in better balance. I created a fluid priority list of all that mattered to me and set a goal to allow myself all of it without causing detriment to myself. Instead of expecting myself to go hard in every area of my life all the time, I gave myself permission to set priorities and to move them around my board of life based on what required my immediate attention at the time, guilt free (I'm still working on the guilt free part, but hey, we all have things that are a work in progress lol). It requires me to be present while I am engaged where I am, and very communicative with all parties so they understand they too will get their turn. In doing this, I'm able to be as passionate about all aspects of my life without depleting myself entirely and putting myself at risk, which ultimately affects many others who depend on me. Nothing is perfect. Please don't be misled. This fluid priority list is mine which means it doesn't always flow with everyone else, but it is what I need to do for me to be happier and at my peak health emotionally, mentally, physically, and spiritually. I continue to work on this and now see it as a core responsibility even in those moments when I don't see my health as the motivation. I realize it's core to my responsibilities as a leader in all of my circles. Going through this and other life-changing experiences, where I made space for me and set better boundaries, has actually made me truly more compassionate and sensitive in all of my roles.

I'm journeying through life as part of a powerful collective. I have been so incredibly blessed in my life to have been raised by parents who made it a priority to create space for my brother and I to dream bountifully, and have provided the necessary vehicle for us to really put ourselves out there. Often when I would tell my father about the exciting opportunities before me, he would respond, "That's on my bucket list or I have always wanted to do that..." and, "I support you completely. You can do anything as far as I'm concerned." My mother told me recently before I left for India to fulfill another calling, "Michie, some people are just made to do great things, built for greatness...when I think about you, I'm reminded of people who can't sit back because they were created to make an impact." My mother, my best everything, has dedicated her life to my brother and I creating a nurturing base, the birthplace from which all of my inspirations and dreams originated. My father, the one who ignites my inner power for greatness, instilled in me that I can make a difference in this world. Be assertive, share your vision, be heard, and the world can't sit back without listening. My husband of fifteen years, who has listened to my laundry list of dreams, often with such unrealistic timelines and effort needed to realize, I would leave him with his mouth open and eyes wide while he responded with an, "Okay babe, if that is what you want to do…" I must admit though that was his initial reactions in our earlier years. As he watched me put in the work to create my own kind of reality and things took shape, his expression changed more into confident smiles and hugs and kisses of congratulations while reminding me to be mindful to replenish myself and to come back to Earth every now and then. We are very opposite in how we approach things of this nature thankfully since it has helped me with my balance. I am forever grateful for his presence in my life. My incredible daughters, aged fourteen, ten, and eight, have also played a significant role in this collective. My three greatest blessings have been such a source of inspiration, motivating me to do what I do. While this certainly true, the contradiction is they have had to adjust the most to me at times being away from our home while I am creating, developing, and executing my dreams. I would say this has been where my best communication skills have been required. How do you explain to your three loves that even though you are going away, or may be busy on task and working long hours, that THEY are the most treasured people in your life? This communication has taken many forms depending on their age and stage, a mixture of expressions. I would say I have learned to gear this to each of their personalities, needs, and levels of understanding. The way I see it is they have been forced to be very generous to share their mama with the world so when I am with them, I need to continue to find ways to show my appreciation for them and their willingness to support me. All parents who have found themselves in this situation will understand. Speaking for myself as a mother, with almost every incredible opportunity that have taken my time, it is often followed by many questions like "What about the girls?" or "How are you going to leave them?" The answer is with a heavy, conflicted heart because I always want to be with them. But If I dismiss following my purpose and using my gifts, I am not a whole wonderful me! I am always praying for guidance from God that I am doing the right things continuing to live out these dreams and for Him to direct my path. I move through life in my faith and trust that He will take me where I need to be when I need to be there. And when He brings me back to my girls, it's a lot of movie dates, walks to the park, short trips, and even time spent in bed all together storytelling and catching each other up that means so much and helps us stay connected. One of my mentors, my older brother has remained someone I lean on when I am trying to sift through my ideas and opportunities. He relates to my drive and dedication like only a pseudo twin can. He's only three years my senior and has never let me fall. His gentle shakes, rattles, and incredible boost ups since childhood have always paved a confident path for me to travel on route to accomplishing my goals. My family, my foundation has been fundamental in making my dreams achievable. Through their supportive actions of being available and resourceful, along with words of encouragement and empowerment, has made all the difference for me. And with this wonderful base to work from, I have been further blessed with an extended network of close friends and colleagues who are quick to offer what they can to support my vision over the years. I am grateful and recognize how impossible it has been for equally driven people who don't have all that I have been blessed with.

So how does one manage life? Start with you. When I came back and started with me, what I found was this: I thought the more I loved on others, the easier it would be to love and accept myself. In truth, the more practice I had loving on others just made me better at loving others and I just kept collecting more others along my journey as I became a master of self-neglect. It's what has led to some of my greatest mistakes; the impact for me has been huge. I had to find what balance meant for me – that which keeps me excited about life, stimulated, and connected. Once I dug into that, there has been no turning back. Ask yourself what does this excavation process look like for you? Maybe it's time to sit with that question first. Just start the process – you have no idea where it will take you. Take this book for example. While I started these words for this compilation typing on my computer, sitting on my bed in my home in Ajax, Ontario, Canada, I'm completing my words at a glass dining table while looking out of a bay window over-looking fields in Mohali, Punjab, India. Once you open the door of your own self-discovery, you never know what you will find between the spokes.

Explore and discover what you love, what fills you and inspires you, and you will uncover where you need to place your life's focus. Design that focus to be your life's mission and feed it into your routine activities. Be proud of finding what is real and true for you and share it with those you love and who love you. Let your passion radiate through you in each interaction and all of your moments. Let this assist you in building your support system, which will carry you as you reach while you climb. Be patient with yourself and others and don't let anyone stop you from dreaming.

Congratulations, you have now created instant passion in all that you do. Like me, that passion will fuel you to be able to DO IT ALL on your own terms and LOVE every magical moment!

Michelle Francis-Smith is a mother, mentor, teacher, doula, and a Registered Massage Therapist who has been practicing massage therapy since 2001. She is an active faculty member and coordinator at Sutherland-Chan School of Massage Therapy Alumni and graduate of the University of Toronto. Michelle is the Founder of ASK MFS Support Services and Co-founder of Perinatal Massage Therapy Education. She runs a busy multi-disciplinary clinic and is currently travelling to Uganda and India, educating on the power of touch. Her thirst for knowledge and desire to empower Massage Therapists with tools for success are what truly inspire her to step into the world.

www.michellefrancissmith@gmail.com

www.pregnancymassagetherapy.com

Compiled by Anita Sechesky

Diamond Glitters of Resilience

"A woman hurts and heals all within one breath. Like a wounded solider, a woman will stand up for her loved ones, regardless of what it may cost her. Always pour out your love and encouragement when you see she is feeling down and distraught. Her low moments never last when she is lifted up by the love of her most precious and dear ones. You are never late with your love."

~ *Anita Sechesky*

Mary Hilty

Diamond Letters

Dear Diamond Sisters;

This is one of those times when we get to line up side by side and thank our lucky stars for our courage, inspiration, strength, determination, and understanding for what being a woman is really all about.

The trials women face are varied and enormous as we are engaged with the challenge of being gatekeepers in our homes and families. I laugh at any reference made to our being the weaker sex. Yes, right...NOT! Women are the backbone of our homes, the strength behind our men, our children, often our communities, and many, many other relationships. We are bookkeepers, housekeepers, mothers, child care providers, PTA participants, lovers, confidantes, counselors, caregivers, and so much more. It is truly amazing that we find any time at all for ourselves and each other. That is one of the best differences we share as being women. We make the time!

We handle our challenges in a completely different manner than our guys. We are more direct, less fearful, or angry. Being mothers or wives prepares us to do battle when there is any war at all waged upon our lives, our homes, or often our gender. Even those of us who do not face the challenges of married life or parenting...we still are shouldering a vast amount of compassion, generosity, and genuine caring for what life brings to us.

"Shine Like a Diamond – Compelling Stories of Life's Victories" is a collection of life stories that polish each and every one of us as we carry whatever comes our way to successful conclusion. In the end, we get it! We have stories of tragedy, jubilation, and triumph. Many of us face sadnesses within our lives and experiences that must be shared so that we can be of benefit to others with whatever it is we have polished up "bright and shiny" in our own life's experiences. As women, it is easy for us to share these things that happen to us.

We are not afraid.

Our strength is the result of shouldering so very much and not really gaining the right recognition for it...except ultimately we are receiving all the recognition we could ever want or need. Looking back over the landscape of the years that comprise our lives, we are reminded that whatever we thought was so horrible back then wasn't really so bad at all. It brought us to a place of peaceful understanding of what kind of warriors we are. It helped us to gain the conviction, the courage, and the wisdom to handle whatever is going to come next. We know there will be more. Some really great and some not so great...but we will be ready.

We have been busy shining up the part of our lives that needed shining. We have done that together as a body of energy strategically honing in on those things we hold dear...those things that hurt so much and taught us some very lasting lessons. It is not easy to keep getting up after we fall and one of the most important truths we will ever gain in this lifetime is "Nobody else is the boss of Me!" At some point within us, a powerful voice screams out that we are important. We matter, we contribute, we care, and we learn from all the difficulties we have faced...that we are tough, resilient, and bright.

Shining Like a Diamond is not easy. We do it because we pick up whatever lessons are being taught and we run with them. We share the information with others and we learn not only what was taught to us through our lessons in life but we learn how to profit from the hard fought lessons of others. This sharing with the world business is important. It is difficult to be vulnerable! The reward is the strength to see beyond the challenges and find ways to use those same challenges as we move deeper into our lives. We can effect change in lives of other people by being courageous enough to share things we keep bottled up inside...things we are afraid of sharing. Once shared, the benefit to others is enormous and that is why *"Shine Like a Diamond – Compelling Stories of Life's Victories"* makes each and every one of us "God Mothers" to all of the others. Give yourself and your experiences a little glow...a little polish and SHINE!

Respectfully yours,

Mary Hilty

Compiled by Anita Sechesky

Winnie Smith

Chapter 14

Hiding in the Shadow of His Wings

Keep me as the apple of the eye, hide me under the shadow of thy wings. (Psalms 17:8) KJV

The devil had a mandate to kill me.

I was always that child who was fearless and would act out physically or emotionally in any given situation. I was not the one to let others walk all over me; I had the spirit of the Archangel Michael. If someone had an issue with another, I came to their rescue. Looking back at moments where I was in Junior Public School helping my teachers in class, I had been ridiculed by class members who were jealous of me helping out.

They would wait for me in the school yard until after class was finished to mock me. They called me "Left hand crab," a name given to individuals who used their left hand to write. Arguing was never my cup of tea. My classmates would say abusive words to me, but I would not pay attention to them. However, the minute they would confront me close up or hit me, that would never go down without a fight. The thing about people who use their left hand is that they are very gifted in many areas. There are many individual who uses their right hand and "can't do it." I happen to remember in school when the teacher would work out the mathematics on the board. I would do it a different way in my books, sitting in my seat, being afraid to go to her with my answers. One day, she finally began to walk around the classroom to see who was doing their work. As she came by, I didn't hide my work because I was positive about the answers I got. She then reassured me that it was okay with the way I worked it out. I was very pleased with that!

When I was about twelve years old, after experiencing the presence of the Holy Spirit, spiritual attacks came on every side. I fell in a cast iron stove, which burned and took out a portion of the flesh on my left calf. I swallowed a piece of metal ball from the toy I was playing with during the Christmas season. I remember crying out to my father to get it out of my lungs. I had great perseverance, even when my father had given up. I went back to him one last time to try again. My father looked into my eyes with great pain and suffering in his to see his child going through this ordeal. Yes he had faith and perseverance as a dad, but did you know that when God has placed some powerful things in you as a parent, your children receives this kind of gift as well? So we are to reach out and grab this inheritance; it's yours to receive. It's in your gene. What I witness is, "Our children inherited gift from us, and their gift become stronger because you have set the pace, in prayer and believing God in your own life for greater things to come, and for Him to sustain our generation." Does anyone know what I am talking about?

Before my mother had passed away in 2013, she had witnessed some things of God in my life. She also witnessed evidence of the evil man in my life. I would pray to God every day when I was under attack and she would see me constantly reading scriptures and observing the power of God manifested in my life. She would hear me repeatedly prophesying about things and people. I discerned good spirits and bad spirits when someone entered my home or we would go out and come into contact with others. "My mother knows me well." She was a humbled soul and we would go everywhere together: weddings, funerals, church, even to visit a friend in their home or in the hospital. She was with me! The bible tells us *"Honor your mother and father that your days may be long upon the Land."* (Exodus 20:12) KJV. God will bless you because of who you honor.

There was never a dull moment in my mom's life during her last days here on earth with us. She enjoyed the last three years of her life wearing the best attire, eating nourishing food, worshipping God together in church with her daughters, grandchildren, great-grandchildren, and her great-great-granddaughter. I am happy to know that she went home to be with the Lord in a royal setting She dance at church the Sunday before she went home to be with the Lord. The Monday she suffered a massive stroke. What happened was that she remembered losing her ring that was given to her by my younger brother, who live far away in Florida. She had not seen him for as long as twelve years. Mom left the kitchen to go up to the room to look for her ring again, even though we didn't find it after many attempts. At that time, she experienced a massive stroke and fell to the ground in the bedroom. I found her gasping for breath with her eyes open. As I tried to lift her up off the floor, she looked into my face. My mom was always saying, "I am not ready to go anywhere," which meant she was not ready to leave this earth. "WE" do not know the day nor the hour when we will leave this earth. Then it dawned on me while laying hands on her at the hospital and praying – the reason why I had ordered this white bridal dress on the Saturday, one week before she had the stroke. I went on the computer to cancel the order, but could not follow through with the cancellation. The dress came during the middle of that week, and then she had the stroke on the following Monday.

My youngest daughter said to me, "Mom, where are you going with this dress? You better sell it." Now as a witness of this act of God, I knew in my conscience that I was led to buy this dress for my mother. I was ordering some bridal dresses for my business and was led to get the size sixteen dress for my mother. It was while she was in hospital and I was praying for her with my sister and daughter present, I heard in my thoughts, "The dress you ordered is for your mom. Jesus is the bridegroom, she is the bride of Christ." I was astonished and call out to my sister, "Oh the dress I bought for Mom is truly hers. I got the revelation about why I ordered the bridal dress." God works in mysterious ways. I wrote this part to let others know that when we are used by God, we must be obedient to his ways and his will in our lives. And when he says to do something, just do it. It is your faith that pleases God. *"Faith without works is dead."* (James 2:14-26) KJV Sometimes, one would say the devil does this or that, but remember, God does use the devil to carry out His works.

The bible tells us in *"Lest Satan should get an advantage of us; for we are not ignorant of his devices."* (2 Corinthians 2:11) KJV We can't leave space for the devil to enter in to harm us. Mom was in the kitchen washing dishes, then she went up to the bedroom looking for the ring. Her blood pressure rose and she fell to the ground, maybe hitting her head. The minute I called her, I said, "Mom, what are you doing?" She answered me, "Looking for my ring." I reminded her not to stress looking for the ring. I then said, "You will find it when you least expect to find it." But as a ninety-year-old-woman, everything she has she wants to keep close to her side. What I was trying to avoid happened.

I learned a true lesson in all of this. While waiting for my family friend in the hospital, I saw many people with cancer. My heart wanted to pray for all to be healed, but the Lord wanted me to obey His will. He has certain individuals whom He has chosen to be healed by the saints that he sends. I am a witness to this action of God. Looking at this Muslim lady across the hall who was vomiting in the garbage bin, I felt sorry for her and had great compassion for this lady. But the devil put something else in my thoughts. He said, "Don't go. Her mother who is the tall, strong woman holding her up will tell you 'No, I don't need your prayers.'" Me, a Christian woman, it's not the first time I would pray for the healing of a Muslim person, but at that particular time, I was deceived by Satan himself. I did not go to pray for that sick lady with the cancer, who was dying and she was pale as chalk. It was right after that I had called my mother at home, asking her, "Mom, what are you doing?" Praying for this sick person, my mom might have been protected from death.

I have had many encounters with individuals for me to pray for them to get their healing, but not everyone will be healed and saved from death when we pray. My own daughter, who has also been through some trial times in her life, I have witnessed many things that she has been through. She even called me up to say, "Mom, you didn't tell me when I became a Christian, I would be going through these trial in my life." We all have been tested at some point in our lives; tested by God and by man. Bob Marley would sing, "Only the fittest of the fittest shall survive. *We go through life with obstacles that help us to grow and to know that we serve a God who is faithful and just. "He will never leave you nor forsake you."* (Deuteronomy 31:6) NIV, in times of trouble. I remember the times when I would walk the house and go into my children's room, replacing the bible that they tossed aside which was given by the public school they use to attend. I would remind them to read the Psalms. That was how I first learned to fight off the devil in his attacks on my life. Another way was giving God praise with the litany of praise I would get from my church sisters at the Catholic Church. Yes, we had bible study night and also prayer meetings too. The priest didn't do it, but there was a group of women in the Church that would have these meetings. Some were even from other parts of the world who attended the Church: Barbados, Trinidad, Jamaica, St Lucia too, including some Canadians. I am a living witness to this in the Catholic faith. My mom, my daughters, and their children walked the Catholic Faith for a period of time, but originally, I had received the Holy Spirit before I experienced Baptism with water. I was the one who was placed by God for a long time until He began to move me out into another realm of the Spirit, Pentecostal. I can say that I was still procrastinating though, having been so loyal to going to the Catholic church. In 1988, I was going with my family, my sister and her children, and other family members. A Christian Ministry was introduced by my children's grandmother for my daughter to attend. She visited in 2004, but never returned until I was in a conversation with her and mentioned for all of us to go visit there again. If I felt the Holy Ghost there, then we would all attend together. Awesome God was in the sanctuary – praise His Holy name! In 2005, we all started to attend the Christian Ministry, where I have experience my true prayer life as a Pentecostal. Joining the intercessors team, I studied and took the test while I was going through excruciating headaches from sinuses and migraines. All of that didn't stop me from passing the test on biblical studies. I pushed through the pain while groaning and pursuing all that was put before my eyes. Praise God!

I remember when I was under some serious attacks, I would go to the mass every day at 9 a.m. none stop because whatever I thought was going on with me or in my life, it would not have been for my harm. Sometimes God pushes us to take the plunge and stand our grounds. The bible says God give us our finger to fight. *"Blessed be the LORD my strength which teacheth my hands to war, and my fingers to fight"* (Psalms 144:1) KJV. *"My goodness, and my fortress; my high tower, and my deliverer; my shield, and he in whom I trust; who subdueth my people under me"* (Psalms 144:2) KJV. Thank God I was obedient to pursue and walk in His ways and His will for salvation for my people, so that they would follow the path of the Lord, even when it was a great struggle to reach the promise Land. In the Scripture when *"Moses called unto Joshua, and said unto him in the sight of all Israel, Be strong and of a good courage: for thou must go with this people* unto the land which the LORD hath sworn unto their fathers to give them; and thou shalt cause them to inherit it." (Deuteronomy 31:7) KJV. I believe my God protected me, under the shadows of His wings (Psalms 91:4) KJV. "I shine because of him who hath not let my enemies to triumph over me." God has call me from an early age. I slipped away, and He got a hold of me once more, to proclaim His works here on earth for such a time as this. Here I am Lord, receptive to do your will.

Winnie Smith is certified as a Duly Registered Minister through Canada Christian College. She is a Faith Leader in teaching the goodness of God, as well as Pastoral care in hospitals and intercessor for souls, healing, and deliverance. Winnie is an online prayer partner for Crossroads Ministry as well as an entrepreneur, Best-Selling Author, and Inspirational Speaker. She is a loving mother of five children and has been passionate about the love of people from a young age. Winnie is an author of four anthology books, including this publication and *"Transforming Lives One Story at a Time"* with Compiler Nikki Clarke.

https://www.facebook.com/winnie.smith.33

http://authorwinniesmith.com

Compiled by Anita Sechesky

Anita Sechesky

Chapter 15

Shining Like the Diamond I Am

When I was a young girl growing up in Northwestern Ontario, Canada, I often daydreamed of what it would be like if I resembled my favorite doll. There she was, just cruising along on the television commercials. All my friends loved her and her entire collection. It was a well-known fact how perfect my little doll was because every girl I knew who owned and played with her was quite excited to have all of her accessories and entourage. I didn't even have blonde hair, but it didn't matter to me. I couldn't believe how much a small plastic doll was loved by all the girls! I just knew it was something big when everyone loves and adores you.

Amazingly, this was one of those major defining moments in my young life because I can honestly say now as I look back I can see where I had started to apply the art of visualization, as technical as this may seem. Many people don't even realize that they are already applying it in their lives. This type of re-framing and concise perspective is a powerful method that I have used as a professional. I have applied this tool to guide my own clients when they have faced challenges in their lives in order to not be discouraged, to set goals, shift mindsets, and achieve success. Yes, I admit it was a whole different aspect of observing my world when I was a child with limited life experiences to glean from, and yet it was the profound "doll" experience that helped me develop a positive mindset.

Amazingly enough at such an impressionable age, and without the influence of others, I made the decision of what I wanted in my life and I choose to focus on it until I achieved it. This was such a strong mindset which I adapted into my persona that nothing which affected me negatively held me back anymore. I knew what it felt like to not really fit into the right groups and to see all the other popular kids doing their own things together. All that mattered at the time was that I had something to hold onto and pull me through when things weren't so beautiful. Even though I was not the most popular girl in school and my physical comparison was quite opposite to my plastic doll, I trained my mind not to focus on those differences. By accepting this obvious fact, I only saw the beauty in my life. I changed a negative into a positive.

I'm an eternal optimist even though I've experienced situations that were not my greatest moments ever. I know what it feels like when you know people are talking about you as you walk in the room. I know what it feels like when you want to be friends with someone, but you don't know how to fit in or what to say to them. I know what it feels like when things don't go as you would have loved it to but your friends were too selfish to make you happy. In retrospect, I can see how the energy going to a particular circumstance was the determining factor of this observation. So basically, if I chose to accept that a past experience happened and it did not discourage me from my goals or did not devalue me as a person to the point of causing me to give up on myself, then it did not have to be categorized as my worst experience ever.

I have chosen to process my life events into certain categories. I have adopted this strategy for quite some time, it's been working very effectively, and I can see how far I have come. The place where I am in life right now has been a continual work in progress. It is not a pit stop or even a bus stop. I may not have all the answers of how and what I am going to do about anything. I have been through many life experiences working as a Registered Nurse and the owner of my established publishing company. I will be honest as I tell you there was a time I thought I knew almost everything about human behavior until I learned more about myself. I took the time to understand myself, why I felt the way I did about certain things, and accept that things have happened through no fault of my own. If things were supposed to happen differently, then I could trust that I might or not know about it when the time was right in this lifetime or beyond. In fact, I have come to appreciate the simple fact that if things turn out a certain way, it was for my best interest because if I was to ponder any further, it would just result in causing me further pain and grief. Therefore, I choose not to stress over it more than I have to, and as you can imagine, being an analytic kind of girl this can indeed be quite a challenging thing to do. Weakness is how we perceive ourselves. Emotions can be our strength or our weakness, it's up to us to determine on which side of the fence do we want to see ourselves over the course of our own lifetime.

One of the greatest lessons I learned was when I understood within my spiritual awakening that I cannot change another human being from being themselves no matter how wrong they may be. It's not my place to even try and change someone's perceptions. I realize that I can guide them through my own knowledge or personal perceptions but they still ultimately have to choose. We all make choices and the consequences that result depend on our actions and reactions. One way to think about this is how we can beautify the situation into something good. I always look for that glimmer of hope when things seem impossible – that there are no challenges, only opportunities to achieve something better than where I am at the moment.

I have always chosen to have beautiful thoughts to create my beautiful life despite what my reality may actually be. This is where I found my greatest strength by not ever allowing my pain to drown me in sorrow so deep that I could not swim out of it. I choose to always see the surface and look beyond what life was willing to show me. I always believed there was more than what meets the human eyes, and perception is easily altered by intention and emotional intelligence. I'm the type of person that does not like to focus on any negative thing in my life. My conviction for living this way is so strong that I refuse to let my painful experiences keep me down for too long. For example, I recall when I wanted to become a Registered Nurse, I very much disliked algebra, math, anything to do with arithmetic in High School and I never gave it the attention I should have. So when I was faced with having to complete an algebra course in my Health Sciences Program, in which I was required to pass with a mark of 90%, you can only imagine how quickly I made myself fall in LOVE with numbers and arithmetic. That meant algebra became the love of my life. I quickly overcame my strong negative mindset to embracing the fact that "I suddenly loved math." I loved it so much because I wanted to be a Registered Nurse. I recall meeting one of my former High School counselors at a community event. I told him that I was pursuing a career in nursing and his short sarcastic response was to laugh and wish me "Good luck!" I went on to not only passed the course, but successfully achieved a GPA of 4.0, and I proved to myself and others that nothing is impossible when you choose to believe in yourself and your goals.

For me personally, I have always chosen to be optimistic and not follow the crowd, meaning that if someone didn't like me or something about me, I chose never to become resentful or behave the way they did. Looking back now, I can see that my mom was my voice of reason, encouraging me to let go of any emotional upsets, disappointments, and hurts caused by people I listened to and believed in. So instead of becoming angry and bitter, she encouraged me to choose forgiveness. As frustrating as it was for me as a young woman growing up, I realized that forgiveness was the healthier and sound-minded approach in this life. The latter was never going to give me back the experiences I longed for and lost, or the ones that weren't fair and if I had allowed myself to react from that place of offence or bitterness towards those who lied or mistreated me, it certainly wouldn't have been such a beautiful outcome. Through some of these life events, I learned that people who wilfully disrespect and hurt others are more messed up and are so caught up in their own issues that they have no understanding of the negative impact they are making on those around them.

We are all responsible for our attitudes and behaviors. We must choose to cultivate a life of gratitude and love towards others. Each and every action and reaction is setting a tone for what life will give us back. I have learned to personally choose my thoughts and emotions towards others carefully. Having my feelings hurt is not a choice in life, but I have discovered that the negative energy associated with bad experiences and people is not a healthy way of living. It will draw you into a dark and demeaning life where you cannot see the blessings waiting for you because you can only focus on the offense. In doing so, the stress becomes compounded resulting in attracting more of the same nonsense. Why would I want that for myself? Life already has its challenges and because we interact with so many individuals, why focus only on certain people when we have a whole world full of amazing souls waiting to be connected to us.

As for me, shining like a diamond means that I have made a choice to focus on my beautiful thoughts which are the facets of a life well-lived in order to achieve the life I desire. I can now say I have always done so and although life is not perfect, it's how I have chosen to see it. I have walked through many unbelievable events where others have tried to wilfully destroy or damage my dreams. Some may have thought they had stolen certain dreams, and even though those dreams may have changed and can never be what they were, I'm sure there's something incredible to learn from those life lessons. I now understand why I never allowed anyone to have that much power and control over my God-given destiny. When you have a dream that guides you into something bigger than yourself, life becomes more that just an opportunity to achieve things. It becomes a deeper spiritual and emotional connection to something greater than who you are.

I strongly believe that all women are connected on a very deep and emotional level. Our lives have value and living in truth requires us to see the priceless beauty in each other and everything around us. The friction that takes places occasionally should never distract us from our higher calling and purpose as we position ourselves for greatness. In fact, they often say that a precious gem must go through a refining process to increase its value, therefore every experience you have walked through has actually made you the beautiful woman you are today. We should always be able to see the beauty and merit in those around us. Truly we are but a reflection of each other, as we were created in a universal sea of love unlimited and in this we will always be.

Anita Sechesky is the Founder and CEO of Anita Sechesky - Living Without Limitations Inc. She is an RN, CPC, Best-Seller Publisher, Multiple International Best-Selling Author, as well as a Law of Attraction and NLPP.

Anita is also the CEO, Founder, Owner, and Publisher of her company LWL PUBLISHING HOUSE.

Currently she has successfully branded 300 International Best-Selling authors in the last three years. LWL PUBLISHING HOUSE is a division of her company, in which she offers coaching, mentoring, motivation, marketing, and of course publishing services for her clients. 2016 marks the addition of two new branches in LWL PUBLISHING HOUSE dedicated specifically to children's books of inspiration and learning, and also fiction and non-fictional single author books.

Working with Anita at one of her "LWL INSPIRED TO WRITE" workshops, Webinars or one-to-one support, will equip you to step out of your comfort zone fearlessly! Anita's solo book entitled "Absolutely You - Overcome False Limitations & Reach Your Full Potential" was written in less than four weeks and she can teach you how to do the same!

CEO of Anita Sechesky – Living Without Limitations Inc., Founder and Publisher of LWL PUBLISHING HOUSE.

Best-Seller Mentor, Book Writing Coach, Registered Nurse, Certified Professional Coach, Master NLPP and LOA Practitioner, multiple International Best-Selling Author, Workshop Facilitator & Trainer, Conference Host, Keynote Speaker.

Join my Private Facebook group: LIVING WITHOUT LIMITATIONS LIFESTYLE.

With over 960 members, we offer exclusive prizes, co-authoring opportunities, Random Contests with FREE Publishing possibilities, "Inspired to Write" Webinar classes, and more - http://bit.ly/1TlsTSm

Please visit our Facebook page: LWL PUBLISHING HOUSE

Website: www.lwlpublishinghouse.com

Email: lwlclienthelp@gmail.com.

Join my Private Facebook group:

LIVING WITHOUT LIMITATIONS LIFESTYLE: Exclusive prizes, co-authoring opportunities and Random Contests with FREE Publishing opportunities. http://bit.ly/1TlsTSm

YouTube Channel: http://bit.ly/1VEGHew

Website: www.anitasechesky.com

LinkedIn: https://ca.linkedin.com/in/asechesky

Twitter: https://twitter.com/nursie4u

Compiled by Anita Sechesky

Mary Hilty

Chapter 16

Can't Forget How Far I've Come

He was a soldier stationed in Germany and I was a high school student. We would exchange long, long letters to each other and talk about our hopes and dreams for our future together. He was gone for an extended time and I was filled with romantic notions as any sixteen-year-old girl would be. He gave me my first engagement ring at sixteen. I wore it to school a few times feeling quite full of myself and then I gave it back to him…waiting for a time when I was grown up enough to be engaged. Looking back, I recall not getting much respect from my teachers and many "oohs and ahhs" from the squealing, giddy friends I had made in high school. In those days, many young girls would marry and many would be widowed shortly thereafter as this was during the last part of the 60's and the Vietnam War. He was fortunate. He never got called into active duty and did his entire stint in Germany. He also learned to drink beer and become a person who had to drink while he was stationed there. My inexperience with alcohol, hookers, and the whole experience he had while in Germany did not prepare me for any of what would come.

I was a girl, really. I married at nineteen…bright, eager with a heart filled with trust and expectation. The whole notion of being one of the first from my high school graduating class to marry filled me with the kind of pride which could only belong to the very young and very inexperienced. I would learn much from my naivety and I would learn very, very quickly.

The reception was big, splashy, and festive…held at the local VFW which could accommodate a rather large guest list. There were six bridesmaids, six groomsmen, a ring bearer, a flower girl...all the bells and whistles, flowers, cake, dancing, DJ, a large, grand feast. There were many pranks done to the Bride and Groom as is the way with Midwestern, rural weddings. And then...it was over. I was Mrs. Somebody and my life was forever changed. Looking back, there is no way I could have realized just how much.

We shopped for furniture. I liked the more modern styles of the day. It was the era of harvest gold, avocado green, and burnt orange. Appliances, dishes, carpet...the works. Of course, I had no individual taste at the time (too young) and I kept with the trends of the day...the colors of the era. We lavishly appointed our two-bedroom apartment with everything a young married couple would need for comfort and for show. Oh yes! We did it up big. Only the best for us! We were young and excited to be Mr. and Mrs. Somebody. Our life together had begun!

I worked full-time job and had this position as a bookkeeper at a paint company during this time. He worked for a company that manufactured stainless steel canisters for the expanding soda industry. Our weeks were full of our jobs, dinners at home, home packed lunches, Sonny and Cher, Laugh-In, visits to both our families, and the ever-growing weekend plans which always seemed to be full of alcohol.

We went out most weekends and danced and had some drinks with friends. As his wife, I could drink in those establishments as long as I was accompanied by my "responsible" husband. At first it seemed to dazzle me with the activity and merriment of the live music, and the people gave me a sense of belonging. I danced and laughed with all of the patrons and the many, many friends we had as a young "hip" couple. After about six months of this, I got tired of it...tired of the bars, the drinking, the lack of other more positive pursuits. I began to stay home while he continued to go out and drink and dance with his friends. I was so trusting and so naive that it never occurred to me that our marriage was headed into very dangerous territory.

He began to change during this time. He actually became quite irritable and cranky with me. He also started to make suggestions about "swapping" with other people he started bringing to our home after the bars would close. Many times, I would already be in bed sleeping. These suggestions met harsh protests from me and before long, what was so morally disgusting to me became my viewing him as a morally disgusting human being. He would push and prod and try to force me to engage in these situations and I resisted until he began verbally assaulting me and finally physically abusing me as a result of my refusal. At first it was a lot of pushing and shoving and that was as far as it got.

I was worried about my marriage and finally had a conversation with my mom about the situation. She promptly paid a visit to our apartment and handled both the immorality of his suggestions along with the pushing, shoving, yelling, and threatening. It was right around this time I became pregnant with my first child.

For the next seven months or so, everything went reasonably well. He would still come home drunk every time he went out and would threaten me if I did not go out with him, so many times, I would go along with him. This would become our routine until my child was born. Once the baby came along, I became a very fierce opponent indeed. I refused to go out because I did not want to leave my child with sitters and spend time with a bunch of drunk people when I could be at home loving my beautiful child and learning how to be a good mother. The night came when he would grab me by my hair and force me to go with him. This is the night that would change everything forever. We went together to a downtown bar, which was on every corner in the Midwest back then. I noticed that he was getting louder and meaner as the evening wore on and I asked him to take me home. He agreed and when I got into the car with him, I remember him backhanding me hard across my face… yelling and swearing at me the whole time until finally I jumped out of the car. It was winter, the roads were icy, and it was very cold outside. In my mind, I would just walk home from there and he would return to his friends and his drinking. But that did not happen. I spent the next hour running from him while he tried to run me down with his car. Yes, I was afraid. I finally made it home and called my mom who came immediately with my stepdad. She saw the mark across my face and waited patiently for him to come home. When he did, she picked him up from the floor and told him to never ever lay another hand on me or she would let him know what that felt like. For two or three weeks, all was well and then the unspeakable happened – my mother died. My child was just ten weeks old.

I think he actually felt my pain and sorrow for some time after because there were no threats, no hits, no suggestions. I hunkered down to mothering my child and being a homemaker. I had returned to work some months before, separated from him, and my life became worker, mother, homemaker, and his became worker, drinker, absentee head of household, and boss of me and all that involved me. He became jealous, accusatory, and vicious. My child was one year old when there was a quarrel one evening and he threw my child, crib and all, at me. That same evening in the wee hours of the morning, I would wake to him making a threat that forged my new beginning.

The next morning, I rented a small U-Haul, packed as much of my child's belongings as I could, packed a suitcase, and set out for my new life without him. I had a great friend who would drive with me on my new adventure and I moved to California.

I was twenty-two years old, had a one-year-old child, and was headed somewhere I had never been with a person I barely knew in order to get as far away from all the pain, disappointment, and violence as I could get. I headed to the ocean in California but my brakes failed on my old Volkswagen in Sacramento. The morning I left, I had $243.00 in cash. I did not have the money to fix my car, but I had enough money to rent a furnished apartment, which I did. My travel companion and I became close and we built a life together that would span nearly eight years. I did not let anybody know where I had gone until I was a legal resident of California. I called and reported my whereabouts…generally.

Those early years were difficult. I had to ride a bus back and forth to find a job, and then I had to ride the bus back and forth to that job. My friend and companion would take care of my child while little by little I built enough savings to fix the car. Once the car was fixed, he (my friend and companion) would find work and we would slowly construct a platform on which to build a life for ourselves and my child.

During this time, I found child care with some nuns at a downtown rectory. I relied on food stamps to live because I could only secure a minimum wage job. Little by little our lives became better, more secure, and we no longer needed to rely on the "system" to live. We moved to a bigger apartment, then a duplex, and finally into a three-bedroom home. We acquired furniture, built a great life with many wonderful neighbors, and all the violence and bad feelings about the old life disappeared.

I discovered some talents and interests from my youth had traveled along with me and I would become adept at homemaking, gardening, and everything in life that is natural. Herbs, spices, natural medicine, homeopathy, aromatherapy; all these things would be pivotal as part of my new life and how it would unfold.

My companion and I stayed together for eight years, building a great life and eventually we would part ways...remaining friends until the end of his life. He taught me much. He helped me to understand my own strength, purpose, and direction. He taught me how to be a great mother, homemaker, friend, and leader in our circle of influence. He taught me to trust my instincts and to share what I knew with others. He taught me the importance of seeking knowledge and gaining insight to take charge of my todays and tomorrows. He taught me strength and confidence in myself and to grow in an ever-changing world.

The next thirty-seven years sped by and along the way I would remarry and give birth to a second child. My companion would stay in contact with me and my "new" family...checking in from time to time to make certain I continued writing, gardening, and pursuing all of my interests with an open mind and an open heart. He taught me that from the deep dark recesses where things as black and dark as coal can change and take another form and amplify life. He stayed with me, guided me, and loved my first child every day of her life. He helped me to never become bitter, and to accept failure and me.

From that very first day, long, long ago, he was teaching me how to Shine Like a Diamond.

Mary Hilty has written extensively through journaling, composing poems, and a variety of articles. She considers her social interactions with people to be one of her greatest inspiration for writing, which she has been doing most of her life. Mary values her collection of wonderful books, and enjoys gardening, preserving all kinds of foods, and leading a natural lifestyle. She is a mother, grandmother, wife, sister, and friend. A favorite dream is to co-create with other authors and leave her "best self" in the world through writing!

Compiled by Anita Sechesky

Diamond Glitters of Faith

"The wisdom in a woman's soul is deep and reflective. She will always carry you within her heart and prayers. If you are blessed to know a woman who cares authentically for you, never let her walk through the lowest of valleys without pouring out your own blessings of positive words of hope, inspiration, and love. It will never be wasted or rejected. Instead you will find your words planted in the soul of endless beauty that reaps an unlimited supply of gratitude."

~ *Anita Sechesky*

Anita Sechesky

Diamond Letters

Dear Diamond Sisters;

If you knew how amazing you are, you would never allow another person to ever hurt you again. You must know the people who belittle and cause destruction in the souls of others are bitter and broken with no love and compassion for themselves. As we show mercy and empathy for those around us, our hearts have a greater purpose to bring healing for everyone. The way people project their emotions is quite often a reflection of what's happening within them. Life is not always how we expect it to be and there are days you may feel like throwing in the towel. It's in those moments that I encourage you to step back and reflect on how far you've already come. Sure, there may still be a long way to go to achieve your goals. But your journey has always shown you the depth of your dreams, even though you still can't see the bigger picture as it beautifully, and yes sometimes painfully, unfolds before you. You will always find your strength within if you seek a higher power such as God, the Creator and Heavenly Father. It's amazing what a simple prayer cried out in times of struggle and surrender can do for your broken spirit and lost soul in a world of hate, contempt, and jealousy.

I implore you to never be hard on yourselves and don't take out your frustrations on the very people who care so deeply for you. They are hurting just as you are when things don't work out as you anticipated. The loved ones we have close to us are the people who feel the deepest desire to see us succeed. Give them a little more compassion and patience for they are not purposely driven by the passion and God source you may be following. In fact, they just believe in you, just as you are. They don't ask questions, instead they just willingly give of themselves to help bring your dreams to life.

It's not always easy to love someone with a deep commitment

for something bigger than self, just like it's not always easy to understand why others are jealous, spiteful, and lacking appreciation and acceptance of who we are.

You will find that life presents you with so many opportunities to connect with multitudes of individuals, but please have wisdom and guard your precious and beating heart. It's in the very moments of inspiring others at their starting points in life that you may stir up something ugly in someone who will never appreciate the knowledge, encouragement, and inspiration you freely pour into them. You see, it's already inside of them Their own ugliness becomes mixed with the jealousy that grows as they witness you striving and jumping over hoops and high towers – you suddenly became a target for competition. They will try to use your naivety and kindness to reap as much information from you. And when things are exposed into your spirit of who exactly they are, they will conveniently lose you to someone else that's up and coming or eagerly looking for someone to follow. Like attracts like, so this is a good thing when you lose those so-called "friends" because they never really were friends. In fact, I would refer to individuals like that as "fiends who suck out the positive energy from you." They glean as much as they can before exiting your life as painfully as possible. Don't let them get that chance to hurt you. Know who they are now and release! Release! Release! Then start focusing on all the love that surrounds you. You are loved and appreciated by so many; why be discouraged any longer by the few who were never meant to be a part of your life. We each evolve and are still growing into our true authentic and loving self. It's your time to continue your journey without any limitations of negativity.

There will come a time when you will see "flashing lights" around certain people I have just described, but unfortunately not until a few have made their way onto your path so you can learn to identify their selfish and false personalities immediately. I have learned quite quickly that when people tell you they were divinely sent to build you up or take you to that next level, it's time to arm all your security systems on the Homefront. From my own experience, they always show up loud, and leave loud and proud. Sadly, they will never achieve what they are after because of their lack of wisdom and integrity. This shortcoming will always hold them back until they make things right and release their own personal past identities in exchange for a clean and clear conscience.

For you my dear sisters of the world, you should know you have the right and freedom to own your emotions, strengths, and creativity. Allow yourselves to be divinely guided and never permit something to block your perception of how to live a life without limitations. You dreamed it and now it's time to achieve it!

With love and gratitude,

Anita Sechesky

Melisa Archer

Compiled by Anita Sechesky

Chapter 17

Diamonds on Ice

At seven years old, I was a very busy child. Mom would drive me around (like it was a full-time job) going to school, participating in swimming classes, Brownies, ballet, singing, and then I fell in love with figure skating. Others did not look upon me as a typical skater. My dad had taught me to skate since I was the age of three. Figure skating was so different, and more structured. I was overweight and other kids had been taking this sport seriously from the time they had learned to walk. Regardless, something inside of me sang while gliding on the ice. It was a different world, so amazing that a person could physically move by gliding and keep their body completely still. Different edges be could utilized, just by a slight lean in one direction or another. Bending at the knees was key. Learning to bend in life lessons is a key, to not falling, also key to sticking a good landing.

My father built me an outdoor rink in the winter. So many cold nights, he would be standing outside to water the ice rink, making it new and fresh. It seemed the entire neighborhood liked to use it. Hockey players would come to enjoy their sport, but leave the ice scarred and tortured, and so very bumpy. How was it fair that I couldn't glide and enjoy the ice my dad had worked so hard on? Learning to share was a hard lesson for me because some things just seemed like they were meant for me. MINE. But others would just help themselves without asking permission or take it for granted that I should share. Often, I didn't understand this type of person because I was always expected to work for what I wanted. Looking back, there was not a lot of free rides. My mantra became *Putting in time and dedication, results in accomplishment.*

I remembered telling my Dad that my feet had outgrown my skates. Then one day, he came home with a surprise: red leather skates with a fur top. I was very excited about these special skates. It was in the 1980's and I had never seen skates that were not white or black.

Proud and excited to go skating for my next lesson night, I wore my red skates with pride. However, it seemed other kids were not as happy for me, as they made fun of my skate color. I wanted new skates and I got them. Who were they to judge me? This event made me more eager to be the best. At first the stares upset me, but soon the stares grew less and less. It prepared me emotionally in a different way that actually helped me more than anything else ever could have. Now singing, dancing, and performing in front of one person or thousands of people, and having the skill to block out stares, allowed me to shine in public.

Quickly my personal self-worth and skating ranking soared as my interpretation to music skills developed. I enjoyed the peace of being lost in translating the music to movement, which improved my competitive edge within my programs. Before long I was taking private lessons. This meant a lot to me as my parents were investing money into my passion and happiness. Other skaters had the same amount time on the ice during the session. However, some kids would just lean against the boards and chat with each other. Realizing the quality of a session relied on my own discipline, it became my drive so that there would be improvement during each session.

Outgrowing my red skates was a very sad time for me, as I conformed to blending in with white leather high-end skates. Soon it became trendy to have tan colored skates. Realizing that others also wanted colored skates was an interesting conundrum. Often the person who is different first, runs the risk of being an outcast, but also stands out from the crowd. Only someone who dares to take a risk and become different can be followed in a trend.

Realizing that there is only one winner in competitions gave me the confidence to accept when I fell in rankings – it lit a fire in me to strive for first place. Soon came a big yearly competition. With no experience in big competitions, I didn't know what to expect. My training took over and my soul got lost in the art of expression to the music. I placed first! My parents got me a nice wooden shelf to put the trophy on. Wow! That is when it really started for me, to be competitive, to feel the achievement of practice and dedication.

My parents asked me what I wanted to do as it was too much money and time to be involved in every activity and I agreed. I focused on figure skating, but continued developing other complimentary skills. I really enjoyed all the different elements. Patch was the quiet time to meditate and train your focus and muscles to trace a fine line on the ice in the shape of an eight. Skills and stroking are the practice of cross over's and footwork. Free skate is the excitement of spins while holding different positions, and jumping to toss your body in the air and spin. It is a very unique feeling, especially tying all these techniques together to create a specific program to compete with.

Dance…I loved dance. There were two different experiences during these sessions. Dancing alone practicing the steps to the music, and dancing with a partner. This was very new to me as I kept trying to lead. It took a lot of patience and dedication from my dance partners to get me to give up dominance. Once I was able to build trust that my partner would not be competitive against me, but rather work with me, the beauty in gliding and turning to music began while building a team.

It was not long before I was traveling to different clubs to compete. I remember watching other figure skaters in my division. Understanding that each jump, spin, and combination were points led me to counting the points and in turn figuring out the final score. With that I realized that my program did not have enough points to win. I then decided that would not do. My coach gave me a good pep talk and I went out to the ice to begin my solo. The music started and something came over me. I went rogue to the program I had spent so many hours perfecting. I added an attempted double salchow, though not quite perfected, but I knew it would get me points for attempting it. I had a quick fall but got right back up and into some fancy footwork I had just added on. Next was a crazy combination of jumps that I have not seen repeated, even to this day, because a flip, a salchow, and toe loop do not start from the same edge. But you knew that. I was so proud of myself to be able to create and succeed at this challenge.

However, getting off the ice was not all cheers. My coach was not very happy about the changes to the routine. I was very excited but there was a shocking discussion as people felt that my teammate was meant to win because it was her time and not mine. This opened my eyes to the politics in the skating world. From there on, I realized that sometimes your best performance may not be enough and I decided to just always do my best. Fortunately, politics did not win out here and I placed first!

My parents surprised me by taking me to a figure skating boutique in Toronto for the most amazing birthday present! They told me I could have anything! Awesome! I got a scribe (this is the tool that makes the circles in the ice for patch), a scribe bag, two pairs of new skates, one for patch as they shave the bottom toe pick off, and a second pair for dance and free skate. Between the victory and my parent's investment, inspiration hit me to become more dedicated to figure skating that led to summers in a local skating school.

The competitions kept getting tougher, but I kept working harder and my trophy shelf filled with ten first place trophies and eight medallions. Deciding to train to be as fit as could be helped me to losing twenty-five pounds in two weeks. My dance coach had pulled me aside saying he was worried about me and asked if I was using drugs. This was so shocking to me. I couldn't even wrap my head around why he would ask such a thing. I guided him outside the arena to show that I was running around the building, rapidly climbing the staircase several times a day, before and after eating. I also showed him the sand hill with the steep side that I sort of jump skied down and then would climb back up, along with jogging the local trail. "Hmmm," I recall him saying. That year I won most improved skater for the second year in a row. This was a huge accomplishment, as I had not heard of someone getting that award in back to back years.

Turning fourteen years old, some decisions had to be made. In order to be taken as a more serious skater, I had the option to participate in a skating school. While skating was a very large part of my life, I needed more. This decision provided me the opportunity to participate in the singing choir at school. Our group won a competition and that took us to the Grand Ole Opry. We got to stand and sing on the stage. This was pivotal for me because as a child my parents took us there to see so many famous singers over the years. If I had only focused on one talent, I would have missed out on other opportunities that ultimately presented themselves to me.

It is imperative to take time to reevaluate your goals and desires. As years pass, you may find more benefit going in a new direction and listening to your heart. As we age, we may not be able to sustain the same passion in accomplishments and we need to make peace with obtainable goals to help us shine.

Training for skating has prepared me for life. You need to make time for different elements such as family, friends, love, arts, exercise, travel, and expression of yourself. Preparations went further to realize sometimes you need to work alone, with partners and sometimes as a team. The best way to shine is to be able to shine under different circumstances, always loving what you do. Others will see your passion as it glows from within you.

Small wins are a necessity! We cannot always be the first-place winner. We can however develop towards our dreams and goals while enjoying the process of building our character along the way to our own personal victories. To strive to be the best is what we all want. To reach for the stars and land in the Milky Way is not devastation, just a different view.

Diamonds are carbon under so much pressure that they create something so clear and beautiful. Most people that are shining like a diamond often have hardships. Everyone has a rough road through some part of his or her journey. People that shine the brightest are those that help teach others how to determine and reach their personal success.

Melisa Archer is the National Trainer for Tesla Wellness Energy. She is dedicated to the wellness of mind, body, and soul certified in: Rejuvenation Facials, Pulsated Electro Magnetic Frequencies, BIO Frequencies, Laser, Reiki level 3, Raindrop Therapy, Vita Flex, Dolphin Neurotism, Healing with Essential Oils, Chemistry of Essential Oils, Sound and Light therapy. Melisa integrates her ability to see and feel energies to better understand her client's needs, and is also eager to train generations on the upcoming movement of electric yoga.

Melisa@TeslaWellnessEnergy.com

www.Electricyoga.ca

Compiled by Anita Sechesky

Sandi Chomyn

Chapter 18

The Hug of Hope

I was in a foster home from the time I was an infant. Looking back, there was a mixture of good and bad experiences.

Up to the age of seven, I did not realize or know I was in foster care until I was told I was moving to a new home and new people that would be looking after me. It was just me moving on, nobody else. Suddenly, I had the sense of uncertainty and confusion. I felt very scared and alone for the first time in my life. It made me think I had done them wrong and they did not want me anymore. I was the bad child.

This new foster mom showed me all of the things she thought and felt I needed to know about household chores. I learned about cleaning, cooking, laundry, and gardening, and was given an education. She told me these were things I needed to know when I was older and would be on my own in the world. I was there until I got married. At the time, it was an escape to get away, as I felt I couldn't make it on my own.

As long as I can remember from an early age, things were always very impersonal in both foster homes. Not knowing any different at the time, I thought it was normal. Even though I saw things were different in other people's lives, I did not question it.

At an early age, did I realize I was learning about different emotions? In my own way, I most likely did but did not recognize them the same as others may have or should have or could have. My classmates called me retarded and teased me about being a foster child. I was always told by my foster parents and teachers that I would not amount to much of anything, because in their eyes they assumed I did not care or was a difficult child and student. In response, I felt like nobody cared about me. I felt I was never good enough in their eyes. I was doing, so I thought, all of the right things or the things they were teaching me to do, but I still felt that they were judging me. Even though I had done everything that I was supposed to do and was told to do. This made it more difficult for me to understand what was going on in my life. This in turn made me defiant as I felt that is what they wanted.

As I was getting older, I was starting to recognize things within myself with mixed feelings. There were many emotions I had that totally confused me. I started comparing myself to others and noticed that I was "different," and my perception of what I felt was normal was starting to make me ask questions. But the questions were only in my own mind, as I felt I should not or could not talk about it. And in reality, at the time, I felt I had no one to turn to.

It was important to know what was happening in my life. I needed and wanted someone to explain the situation to me in a way that I could understand, someone I could trust and talk to about things. But I never had that, and then just pulled away in many ways.

In my late teens, I was assigned a new social worker. When she came for scheduled visits, she took time with me. Suddenly, my opinions were important to someone. There were times she even asked me for advice. It was the very first time in my life that anyone seemed interested in me and my opinion. It helped me to start feeling confident in myself and to see that I had important things to share. She understood my needs, abilities, and capabilities. We worked together on my school work, and together we built up my self-esteem. I started to be proud of who I was and know that I was a beautiful person. The relationship with my social worker provided me with stability and helped me to feel less afraid. I didn't change overnight. It was and still is an ongoing growth. Maybe that social worker is reading this right now. I would like to say thank you as I did not get a chance back then.

She had moved on to new things in her life.

My biggest turning point was a lesson learned from my fiancé's mother. I had gone to the city with my future husband to go shopping and to the summer fair for the day. We then went over to his parents' place for the evening meal and for a visit. As we were getting ready to leave and chatting at the door, my fiancé's mom reached out and gave him a big hug. As I was standing there waiting to go she turned to me and enveloped me in a big hug that had me in shock. I had never been hugged like that before. I stood there not knowing how to act or feel about it. Yes, I had been hugged by my boyfriend, but never from anyone else.

My fiancé's mom felt there was something missing when I didn't return the hug the same way she had given it. She looked at her son and asked what was wrong in her native tongue. Her son wasn't sure what to say. They both looked at me for an answer, which I wasn't sure I could give them.

Without saying much as it was an awkward situation, we let it go. I didn't though. I did a lot of thinking about it the next few days and weeks. I had a lot of mixed feelings about it because I wasn't someone who would talk about it, I internally processed it.

Days and weeks passed and I was to visit my fiancé's parents again. I still felt intimidated and unsure. We had our visit and were getting ready to go. Standing at the door my fiancé's parents gave him his hugs and "I love you." I was standing there waiting. When they were done; instead of them reaching out to me, I reached out and gave both of his parents a hug. I thanked my fiancé's mother for teaching me something special that day of the fair. I then explained to them that I didn't receive hugs growing up, and that it was something new for me. She asked me why I had never been hugged. I told her what I only knew. I mentioned that I was a foster child and that they never showed the emotion to me like they did to their own children. Saying to her, somehow in my mind I thought it was normal but down deep knew it wasn't normal to even think the way I did. She said, "That was so wrong." We talked more about it through the years. For opening up to her, I was wrapped in the arms of a hug by my fiancé's mother.

This was the start of many more hugs and "I love you's" to come.

My fiancé, at the time, also taught me someone did care about me and that I was more than good enough in their eyes. He always told me I am capable of doing anything I want and being the person I want to be. Through his love and understanding and not judging me, I have become that person. I have taught my own children that these two things are very important. They do not leave without receiving and giving hugs and saying, "I love you." All phone calls are ended with, "I love you." Yes, I do work at it continuously. I am very happy to say I have been now been married for over forty years and now have an endless supply of hugs!

Yes there is much we will learn on our own, but it is experiences like this that make us the people we are meant to be. So keep your eyes and ears open for them. If we did not have life lessons that unfold this way when we least expected them, we may not have been able to grow into the people we are today. There are many, many more events like this that can happen for you and me too. I have experienced other life lessons and I am sure you have also. Just let them happen. Yes, you too, like me, can shine like a diamond.

Sandi Chomyn is an International Best-Selling Co-author and Life Coach known as a Life Management Coach. After raising her three boys, she received her coaching training with Coaching Cognition. She's a farm mom and grandma, inside and out, and has come to enjoy the different facets of her life by integrating her life coaching business and her love for scenic photography with good country living. Sandi resides with her husband Bill in a small farming community in Togo, Saskatchewan, Canada.

facebook.com/meetsandichomyn

facebook.com/sandichomyn

Compiled by Anita Sechesky

Diamond Glitters of Peace

"A woman's insight is based on her emotional make-up. The more she allows love to rule her heart, the stronger her intuition becomes. As she grows in her emotional and spiritual journey, there is more peace to be found within all things in her life. No longer do petty and frivolous situations take over her destiny. Hers is to create love and healing everywhere she goes. This gift of peace is not easily achieved and must be nourished with health and well-being at all times. It is the foundation of all things positive and loving."

~ Anita Sechesky

Compiled by Anita Sechesky

Susan Lawrence

Diamond Letters

Dear Diamond Sisters;

I knew I was different as a child for I would always follow my own spirit. Mother said even when I arrived at twenty-seven weeks' gestation, she could see the strength of my fighting spirit when it was thought that I would not make it. She knew that I would.

You see, it takes courage to stand alone in a crowd and not mingle in with the rest. Words of advice: Lions do not lose sleep over the opinions of sheep.

Uniqueness has its beautiful place in allowing it to set you apart from the masses.

There is comfort in knowing that you have within yourself pearls of wisdom from your very unique experience of saying to yourself that you can never be like those who made the choice to give up and walk away.

Be of courage in standing in your very own authentic power, trusting your inner guidance, intuition, and wisdom, for there is no greater teacher than this.

Your soul knows its Truth.

Just by your experience alone of being different, you will RISE. Of that I am positive.

You see what your mind can perceive, one can achieve.

MINDSET is a powerful thing.

Shine Like a Diamond-Compelling Stories of Life's Victories

Compiled by Anita Sechesky

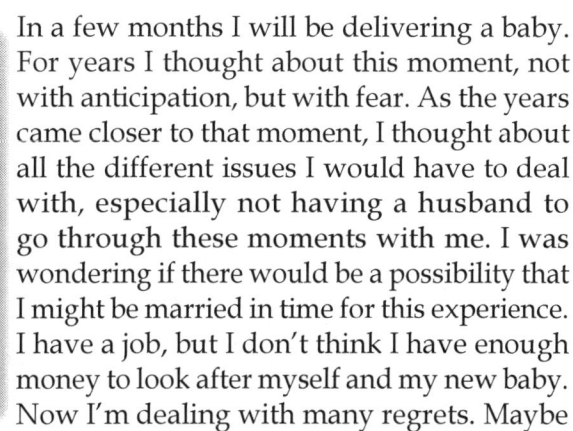

Yvonne Reid

Chapter 19

Pregnant At Forty-Nine

In a few months I will be delivering a baby. For years I thought about this moment, not with anticipation, but with fear. As the years came closer to that moment, I thought about all the different issues I would have to deal with, especially not having a husband to go through these moments with me. I was wondering if there would be a possibility that I might be married in time for this experience. I have a job, but I don't think I have enough money to look after myself and my new baby. Now I'm dealing with many regrets. Maybe if I had really planned for this, because my vision is somewhat foggy, I just can't see what I have accomplished for this moment to be successful. What I mean is when this baby comes, I should have some kind of peace and security that all will be well. It seems as if there was so much wasted time. I wish I didn't. I wish I did. What if? Now it's too late. I cannot change the hands of time, which has caught up on me. Did time cheat me, or did I cheat on time? Some days I thought maybe I could just put this off until tomorrow. I was going to take a nap which turned into a long sleep, and suddenly tomorrow was gone and I didn't finish the book. The gym was put off for another day which turned into another month until the New Year came with a new resolution. Time, you certainly did not wait on me. It was as if I closed my eyes, opened them, and there I was – pregnant at forty-nine. Where did time go?

"So teach us to number our days that we may get a heart of wisdom."
Psalm 90:12

I can feel the baby kicking and stretching my skin, and I can just image the stretch marks that will eventually turn into winkles. My breast will begin to droop and with all of these thoughts, I know it won't be too long before the stress causes my hair to become gray. I looked in the mirror and wondered how the world would expect me to look Magazines have a totally different image of a pregnant woman. I'm certain that will not be able to keep up all the walls and facades people build up over time. Is anybody gonna love this body after all it has being through? I'm gaining weight in all the wrong places. Will I be able to enjoy having sex after this baby comes? Will anyone want me with this baby? Dear God, I don't mean to sound this harsh. Forgive me if I'm complaining. But the media don't make women having children at forty-nine excited. With all these plastic surgeries, women look like Barbie and the men look like Ken. Plus, all the super expensive cosmetics that you would need to purchase as well. On top of that, being called names like "Over the hill," "Ma'am," or "Miss." Where I am going with this pregnancy, as if I can abort it? The only option for me to rid this pregnancy is my death and that is impossible. This baby is a must. There is no going around this pregnancy. I must go through with this and I have two choices: either I embrace it and celebrate every moment of it, or I reject it and live the rest of my life miserable, unproductive. and purposeless.

"And so Sarah laughed to herself thinking, "Now that I've become old, will I enjoy myself again? What's more, my husband is old." Genesis 18:12

Suddenly I looked in the mirror and realized that I wasn't just a woman. It was my mirror of strength and security. There was hope in that mirror. It spoke back to me and reminded me that I am a woman of God, a daughter of the King of Kings. I am made in the image and likeness of God. I am His masterpiece, the apple of His eyes. Suddenly I laugh because I know who holds my future in His hands. My laughter has turned into joy. I am clothed in peace and serenity. My baby is coming and here I am thinking that I wasn't ready…allowing all these negative words to go through my mind. I was visualizing our culture, comparing myself to others around me, and beating up on myself and at that moment, not seeing the woman on the inside of me. I am ready! I have all I need to make the best of my next decade with her. Since I have entered this earth, my experiences have been some good and others bad. Wisdom grew in me over the years. She taught me many things, like learning to make peace with myself, putting value on myself, accepting myself, trusting my decisions and my choices. I look back now and I realize that this baby will bring the most pivotal moment in my life. It is a new beginning; the opening of a new horizon. I put my two feet together, stretch my arms out wide, and I fall back without looking back. Because I know who is there to catch me. I am safe.

"And Moses was an hundred and twenty years old when he died: his eye was not dim, nor his natural force abated." Deuteronomy 34:7

I am entering this new milestone shining like a diamond. Looking in the mirror and feeling good, feeling vibrant, I see the God in me that is helping to create radiance that only He can give. I have a spirit full of life. He is the motivator of me, keeping a smile on my face even at my worse moments. I have learned to speak life into every situation and to be patient to see the manifestation of positive speaking. Taking care of my body, exercising and enjoying the sun, eating and drinking lots of green juices, taking my vitamins and mineral. I have special days to meet up with friends that already had their babies, or are about to. I promise my baby that we will go places that we have never gone before .

"They will still yield fruit in old age; They shall be full of sap and very green." Psalm 92:14

My baby's name will be "Fifty." Yes, as I write this chapter, three months from now I will be fifty years old. I embrace this moment and I give God thanks for extending to me more life. I thank Him for every day of my life and for all my experiences that made me stronger for me to be the woman I am today. In my weakness, He gave me strength. In my struggles, He fights for me. In my life, I've been there and done many things. I can look back and said my great accomplishment was having five children and two glam-children. Yes, I am a glam-mother. And I am also going back to school to accomplish my goals. My greatest accomplishment was to accept Jesus Christ as my Lord and Savior. He allows me to find and create beauty on the inside of me through His words. There were times in my life that I was a quitter; I gave up on things easily. I didn't know how to face challenges. I was a runner when it came to solving problems – always running away from my problems and finding that I had to face it one way or the other. Going back to school was very difficult for me as an adult. So I prayed and I told God that I am always quitting and unless He helped me, I was going to quit. God helped me to accomplish my Grade Twelve, my Bachelor in Theology, and Masters in Divinity. It doesn't stop there because I am interested in being a dietician and a fashion designer. As I reminisce on this new birth, I imagine the freedom. I am liberated, free to do and to be who I am. All my goals and accomplishment came through the beauty of knowing Christ, which is the driving force behind who I'm today. The more I am becoming like Him is the more life issues becomes easier to deal with. It is the more I shine from within.

"A gray head is a crown of glory, it is found in the way of righteousness."
Proverbs 16:31

If there is one person in my life who will help me to have a safe delivery and take care of this baby it will be an eighty-three-year-old woman named "E."

I really don't know if "E" realizes that she is one of my greatest inspirations. Having a friend who has carried and delivered many babies is of great importance in such a vital moment of my life. I remember her announcing to me that she was going to get married at eighty-three to a forty-year-old man. I asked her so many questions to see if this was the right thing she was doing. I didn't really agree with it, but who was I to question her decision. First of all, she didn't look her age. This women was exceptionally beautiful, very intelligent, was still running a business on her own, and going to school at eighty-three. She drives four hours back and forth to go to school on Thursday nights to study Greek. She is also strongly involved in ministries at her church. We always heard that age was just a number and she proved to me that it was. She is a very active woman, eats healthy, and puts on her makeup well. She wears the most beautiful dresses. She taught me that age should not stop anyone from accomplishing their goals and enjoying life. She has been a great support to me by the wisdom she deposited into me. My baby will be fine. My baby "Fifty" will shine.

"Whatever your hands find to do, do it with all your might, for there is no activity or planning or knowledge or wisdom in Sheol where you are going." Ecclesiastes 9:10

The question that I ask myself is: What can I do when I am dead?

Should I have to go to my grave with my dreams? Should I add to the grave yard the many books that were never read, the races that were never run, the buildings that were never built, or the recipe that was never shared? My answer is "No." God has created us all with purpose. I would imagine that the first part of my life was to have things planned out; to create a blue print; to put together a structure and to educate myself for the second part of my life. This is the time for the plans to be executed. This is the time that nothing should be left undone – the bucket list should be cleared up.

I am looking forward for my delivery. As "Fifty" enters my life, she will be clothed in purple, because she is royalty. I am prepared for a life of excitement and uncertainty. To be known as a woman filled with joy and laughter and as people enter my proximity, it will be contagious with love. The God that I nourish in me by my prayers, worship, and His words will be seen in me and brings me favor, blessings, longevity, prosperity, and health from all parts of the earth. I will shine; my gray hair will glisten, and my wrinkles will remind me that antiques are expensive. My focus will be no longer on the outside but the inside where my peace will be. I will blaze trails and history will record me as a woman who is always shining. Yes, she shines like a diamond and, Yes, age is but a number.

"For I know the plans I have for you, declares the LORD, plans to prosper you and not to harm you, plans to give you hope and a future." Jeremiah 29:11

Yvonne Delzine Reid was born in Clarendon, Jamaica and migrated to Canada at a young age. She is the proud mother of five beautiful children and two grandchildren. Yvonne suffered a terrible accident which left her temporarily disabled in 2010, yet she registered into the Assessment Program at Centenary College, graduating with her grade 12 equivalent. In 2011, Yvonne became a full-time student at Canada Christian College, where she studied Theology and also was hired as a full-time worker, and then Maintenance Manager at the college. Yvonne graduated in 2014 with her Bachelor of Theology and then 2016 with Master of Divinity.

CONCLUSION

Thank you for reading our beautiful book. It is my greatest desire that you have been enlightened with the essence of what it takes to "Shine Like a Diamond" and what it really means to the female spirit. "Shine Like a Diamond – Compelling Stories of Life's Victories" is a highly sought-after book and is successful because all my co-authors, including myself, share our own ways of finding strength and courage to achieve the life we all seek, despite what dreams were broken, lost, or stolen from our lives at our most vulnerable times. It has given us each a life full of unlimited potential and triumph we never thought possible at one time. Also, by choosing to have an attitude of love and peace, it has helped us to discover health and wellness on our journey of continuing to be productive members of society, refusing to remain emotionally stuck in our crippling situations, but seeking the confidence we each needed in our most destructive of life's circumstances.

My intention with this powerful all-female cast of contributors was to inspire you to reassess your own life and how you may have allowed past experiences to affect the life you are living today. With so many stories and empowering perspectives revealed in this book, it would be something to see how we can all change the world with just a little more love, peace, and unity, one woman at a time. Women create life within our wombs, and the Universe is also there from the time of our very conception. We are the world we aspire to be, the world aspires to be healed and helped by life-givers – such is the heart and soul of a woman. I encourage you to give up the things that have hurt you or held you back in your own life. Allow yourself the authorization you need and let go of your own individual confines within your soul, as you continue to ponder the wisdom and life experiences of all our contributions. We have all eagerly permitted you into our world regardless of how painful and hurt our feelings have been through various conditions that ultimately led us to find the hope we needed to carry on.

The wealth that is within our gorgeous book is eternal. Just like gold never loses its value, the many perspectives of what "Shining Like a Diamond" means to each of us is tenderly poured into each chapter. This kind of insight alone is enormous and worthy of examination and application in one's day-to-day life.

As the CEO, Founder, and Publisher of LWL PUBLISHING HOUSE, I have supported and mentored all my clients successfully and would love to help you also become a Best-Selling author. In doing so I have managed, coached, and organized several groups of international Best-Selling co-authors in the last three to four years, and have now published this tenth anthology. That's 300 people from around the world who are now recognized as leaders and experts among their peers, as they choose to step into their own achievement and recognition!

Now, my question to you is: "Do you have a dream of writing your own beautiful book? Do you want to inspire, motivate, and encourage others? Do you feel your story and vision can help others to live a life without limiting beliefs and roadblocks in their own lives? Have you gone through something that is so incredible and know that many need to hear your story?" I would be honored to guide and coach you into compiling and writing your own life-changing anthology if you are a visionary that believes in yourself, but just need that professional direction to pull it all together. What are you waiting for? Contact me and let's discuss what your next steps would be to become one of LWL PUBLISHING HOUSE's newest International Compilers.

My company is offering incredible single author packages as well as Children's book authoring opportunities through LWL KIDz. Our Best-Selling books are listed within the categories of self-help, healing, relationships, faith, and positive psychology to name a few.

I would love to help you organize, manage and Publish your book project, as it's also considered an entrepreneurial success step to brand building your business through a book.

Compiled by Anita Sechesky

I have learned so much about people and what makes them inspired and motivated from twelve years of specialized experience as a Registered Nurse and almost twenty years in health care, as well as my extensive training to become a Certified Professional Coach, Living Without Limitations Conference Host and Founder, and of course Best-Seller Publisher, just to name a few.

I understand the frustrations and stress of trying to write your own book. My professional LWL Support Team and I want to assist you in making your dreams and goals a reality as a published author and I want to show you how to do it as quickly as possible. Together we will develop a "Master Plan template for your publishing success." Our goal at LWL PUBLISHING HOUSE is about bringing your vison to life in print.

Anita Sechesky

CEO of Anita Sechesky – Living Without Limitations Inc.,

Founder and Publisher of LWL PUBLISHING HOUSE a Division of Anita Sechesky – Living Without Limitations Inc.

Best-Seller Mentor, Book Writing Coach, Registered Nurse, Certified Professional Coach, Master NLPP and LOA Practitioner, multiple International Best-Selling Author, Workshop Facilitator & Trainer, Conference Host, Keynote Speaker.

Join Anita's Private Facebook group: LIVING WITHOUT LIMITATIONS LIFESTYLE. With over 960 members, she offers exclusive prizes, co-authoring opportunities, Random Contests with FREE Publishing possibilities, "Inspired to Write" Webinar classes, and more - http://bit.ly/1TlsTSm

Please visit Anita's Facebook page: LWL PUBLISHING HOUSE

Website: www.lwlpublishinghouse.com

Email: lwlclienthelp@gmail.com

Join Anita's Private Facebook group:

LIVING WITHOUT LIMITATIONS LIFESTYLE: Exclusive prizes,

co-authoring opportunities and Random Contests with FREE Publishing opportunities. - http://bit.ly/1TlsTSm

YouTube Channel: http://bit.ly/1VEGHew

Website: www.anitasechesky.com

LinkedIn: https://ca.linkedin.com/in/asechesky

Twitter: https://twitter.com/nursie4u

Compiled by Anita Sechesky

Shine Like a Diamond-Compelling Stories of Life's Victories

Compiled by Anita Sechesky

Made in the USA
Middletown, DE
30 May 2017